SOCIAL
MEDIA⚡

SOCIAL MEDIA

FACEBOOK, TWITTER, AND THE MODERN REVOLUTION

LIGHTNING
GUIDES

"Technology and social media
have brought power back to the people."

—MARK MCKINNON

When US Airways Flight 1549 crash-landed into the Hudson River in Manhattan, it took only four minutes for the Twittersphere to begin reporting the news. Flickr had photos in minutes, YouTube had dozens of videos of the crash, caught on mobile phones by curious onlookers, and Wikipedia was updated almost instantly. By contrast, it took more than a quarter of an hour for traditional news outlets to post their first stories. This is the rise of social media, of instant access, of citizen journalism and crowdsourced information. It's grumpy cats and baby photos, but it's also hard news and public activism, a weapon against the oppression of governments and the censorship of knowledge. Social media is the right to a voice, to free speech, and to public assembly. It is, above all, the democratization of information, the hyperfragmentation of distribution, and the power of Now.

CONTENTS

INTRODUCTION

on't shoot the messenger. That's a handy rule. Plutarch wrote about it nearly two millennia ago, and Shakespeare riffed on it in *Henry IV* and *Antony and Cleopatra*. It means that if the news makes you unhappy, don't blame the person who delivered it to you. Or, for those of us who live in the present day, don't blame the app.

It seems like the only thing that has spread more quickly—and taken hold of our society more fiercely—than social media platforms like Facebook and Twitter, is the debate over social media platforms like Facebook and Twitter. Are they good or bad? Do they make our lives easier, or are they slowly corroding our souls?

But social media is just a messenger—an incredibly powerful, catchy, global messenger. Sometimes it's nothing but cat videos and baby photos. (So many baby photos.) But it can be incredibly productive, too. Social media has been a powerful force for propaganda and an efficient means of grassroots organization. It allows equal opportunity for bullies who digitally harass their victims and for those who rally life-saving support for people in need.

Facebook and its friends aren't going away. Millions of people get their news headlines from Twitter, discover new favorite shows on YouTube, or find old classmates on Facebook. So let's not shoot the messenger. Social media is—and always will be—exactly what we make of it.

1990s "SOCIAL MEDIA"

THE FIRST KNOWN
use of the phrase

Social media started from THE BBS (BULLETIN BOARD SYSTEMS), **IRCS** (INTERNET RELAY CHATS), **& USENET GROUPS OF THE 1980s & '90s.**

FACEBOOK
WAS ORIGINALLY RESTRICTED TO
HARVARD UNIVERSITY

ONE OF THE FIRST SITES *that allowed user profiles* **& FRIEND INVITES APPEARED IN 1997.**

What is social media?

Social media is a form (or variety of forms) of online communication—usually via a website or app—that allows users to create virtual communities, share information, network, and connect with one another.

What is a hashtag?

A hashtag (or hash tag) is a label or type of metadata that can be added to a social media post. It is a word or phrase, without spaces, preceded by the number sign (#), also known as a "hash sign" or "hash mark." Hashtags are searchable and used to categorize posts by topic as well as to add commentary both humorous and serious. Hashtags were vital to organizing online movements like Occupy Wall Street. The hashtag was first used on Twitter but has since spread to other social media platforms.

Does using social media give companies your data?

Social media sites like Facebook make their revenue not from their users, but from advertisers who pay top dollar for information that lets them target customized ads based on personal data. As a result, social media sites encourage users to add as much information as possible to their profiles. Social media may give big companies your data in exchange for a more personalized user experience that facilitates social connections. Social media sites do have privacy policies, and users should investigate the policies to customize and enhance privacy protection settings.

What is location-based social networking?

Location-based social networking, or "geosocial networking," tags user posts by cities, towns, and neighborhoods, and allows users to "check in" to locations. The best-known location-based social media platform is Foursquare, but other sites and apps have added location-based functions. Instagram, Twitter, and Facebook allow users to include location data with posts and images.

What use is social media?

Aside from letting people share cat videos and pictures of their new grandchildren (perfectly good uses in many people's eyes), social media is employed more and more by businesses large and small. It is increasingly part of a powerful marketing strategy (or a good way to fail at marketing, depending on how it's used), a way to develop business contacts, and an effective means of connecting with customers. Social media is also powerful at organizing people widely separated by geography but united by interests.

How does social media help people?

Social media is a powerful tool for connecting and engaging people who might otherwise feel isolated. Campaigns for social justice and political protests have been organized on Twitter; Facebook users have rallied to find missing people; Tumblr has sprouted blogs devoted to exposing the sexism inherent in so much of popular culture, and showing the major roles played by people of color in medieval European history, as well as educating readers about evolution, museums, and a vast array of other topics.

PROPAGANDA

A BRIEF HISTORY

F orms of social media are as diverse as the people using them. One such way, however, stands out as particularly controversial: social media as a platform for propaganda. Propaganda is communication with a purpose: to convince and indoctrinate. It serves a cause, it's manipulative and characteristically biased, accounting for its negative reputation.

The term "propaganda" was popularized during World War I, but the techniques have been around since the onset of human interaction, albeit at a smaller scale. The word itself first appeared in 1622, when Pope Gregory XV established a council for spreading the official and approved doctrines of the Catholic faith. He called this group the Sacred Congregation for Propagating the Faith, *Congregatio de Propaganda Fide* in Latin.

RED, WHITE, AND BLUE REVOLUTIONS

Although the word "propaganda" was not widely used at the time, the principles of propagating were put into vigorous use in the late 1700s and 1800s during two historical events: the American Revolution and the French Revolution.

Left: A dance performance featuring a banner with the rallying cry of the 18th-century French Revolution "Fraternity, Equality, Liberty", Berlin, 1958.

In 1765, the American colonies opposed the British rule, particularly on account of taxation, and decided to remove the British officers from their land, a move that did not find all citizens in agreement. A propaganda campaign was used to spread the idea that American residents should not have to pay taxes to a distant government in which they had little say. The slogan "No taxation without representation" kindled the flame of revolution, and the campaign to recruit revolutionary support was met with high success. By 1783, the British recognized American independence, and the United States became its own country.

That revolutionary fervor, immortalized in historical documents and declarations, eventually found its way across the Atlantic and inspired the French to revolt against their rulers. Leaflets and posters that later became part of the Western art historical canon fueled and kept alive the French people's passion for overthrowing the *ancien régime* for an entire decade, from 1789 to 1799. The ideas of liberty, equality, and solidarity—distilled in the slogan "*liberté, egalité, fraternité*"—spread throughout Europe and gave rise to what we now refer to as modern liberal democracy.

CAMPAIGNS, NOT CONTROL

An important distinction should be made between propaganda and other types of campaigns. Though many ideological,

Slogans like those used in the American and French revolutions are tools of propaganda. They condense sometimes-complex ideas into simple and profound catchphrases. Other instruments of propaganda include: humor—poking fun at opponents in a cartoon, for example; symbolism, like Uncle Sam representing the United States; and endorsements, especially from well-known figures.

political, or even advertising campaigns use the same basic techniques as propaganda, the difference lies in the execution of those techniques. While any movement might create its own slogans and arresting imagery, propaganda exaggerates beyond the point of reality. Take, for example, the abolitionist movement in the American South. In sheer number of victims, excess of brutality, and duration, no institution has equaled the transatlantic slave trade, which saw countless Africans captured, sold, and killed.

The movement, which spread emancipatory ideas through pamphlets and posters, exemplifies a savvy campaign that brought the shocking conditions of slavery to light, but stopped short of propagandizing.

A particularly evocative example was the much-reproduced image by Josiah Wedgwood (of the Wedgwood ceramics family) of a black man in chains and a caption that reads: "Am I not a man and a brother?" Photographs of slaves showing horrific scars from beatings and depicting the cruel conditions of their captivity were also frequently used, with outstanding effectiveness.

In 1780, Pennsylvania became the first US state to abolish slavery. Other states followed, then other countries. The idea that freedom and equality were inalienable human rights had begun to go viral.

WORLD WAR I

Although the techniques were already in effect, the term "propaganda" was not commonly used until World War I. Known at the time as the Great War, World War I saw propaganda's rise to an art form.

World War I was instigated by the assassination of Archduke Ferdinand of Austria, but it was actually the result of years of political and economic rivalry among the world's most powerful countries. Some of these nations—Great Britain, Russia, Austria-Hungary, and others—were globe-spanning empires, and the resulting clash was immense. But, like most wars, World War I was not fought only on the battlefield: it was also fought with ideas and emotions, by spreading lies and truths, as needed, to stir up public support.

The American fictional character Uncle Sam, for example, was used extensively to symbolize the country's nationalistic feeling. Posters featured a white-haired patrician who resembled Abraham Lincoln pointing at the observer and exhorting them to support the effort by enlisting, buying war bonds, or offering any other kind of help.

THE RUSSIAN REVOLUTION

Russia suffered by far the biggest human casualties of World War I; it also found itself in complete financial devastation. By 1917 the Russian people had had enough of Czar Nicholas II and his ineffective and pompous rule, and the Emperor abdicated his position. In place of the old regime, a provisional government was formed, but it was not much better at repairing the country's broken economy than the czar and his government had been.

Only a few months later, the provisional government itself was swiftly overthrown by the Bolshevik party, led by Vladimir Lenin. The Bolsheviks created the world's first Marxist government, with Lenin as their leader.

While propaganda played an important role in the Russian Revolution, it was especially instrumental in maintaining support for Lenin's government and promoting socialism to Russians. The Union of Soviet Socialist Republics (the USSR) soon formed, and the key to Soviet power was advertising the notion that Communism was the best possible social organization. Nationalism—bolstered by patriotic slogans, fabric designs with images celebrating workers, and posters extolling Soviet industry—was the glue that held the Union together in the face of the West's increasing efforts at democratization.

MASTERS OF PROPAGANDA

No other case exemplifies the power and effectiveness of propaganda better than Germany's Nationalist Socialist Workers' Party, a. k. a the Nazi Party.

Germany had been left wounded at the end of World War I. It was in economic

DID YOU KNOW

The Russian Revolution was actually two separate revolutions. The first, known as the February Revolution (so named because Russia still used the older, Gregorian calendar instead of the Julian calendar used by the west, which puts it in March), was the overthrow of the czar and the royal family. The second, the October Revolution (which happened in November by the Julian calendar), was the overthrow of the provisional government by Lenin and his Bolshevik party.

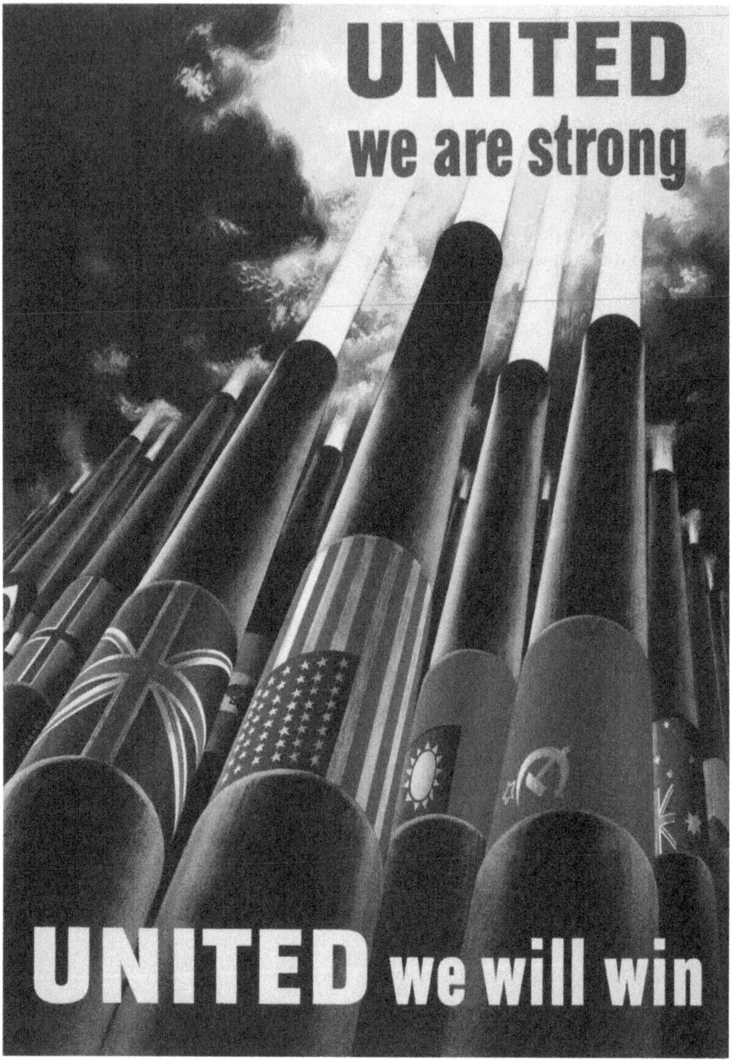
UNITED
we are strong
UNITED we will win

ruin and had to pay reparations to many of the countries it had fought against. As it always happens, it was the German people that bore the brunt of the country's economic woes. Germany's propaganda machine scapegoated other countries for all the problems that Germany was facing, framing the plight of the people in an "us versus them" rhetoric where good, hardworking Germans were the victims of British and French neo-colonial aggression.

But Hitler didn't stop at simply stirring up nationalistic sentiments of millions of Germans. Once he found himself in power, Hitler started haranguing about German purity: true Germans were members of the master race, known as Aryans. Jews deviated from this pedigree and as part of Hitler's megalomaniac campaign to "purify" his nation, they were subjected to one of the most ferocious genocidal campaigns in modern history. The Nazis perfected the 'art' of fearmongering, but by the time the world realized the bloodshed and destruction afoot, the damage had already been done.

But propaganda was not only used by the Nazis. It was used by both sides of the World War II countries to recruit soldiers, bolster morale, and spread fear and suspicion about the enemy. The growing popularity of the radio was used by both the Allies and the Axis to try and convince the rival side that defeat was impending while also giving their own troops hope that the conflict would soon come to an end.

PROPAGANDA NOW

Today, we have grown accustomed to the idea that almost all the information we could possibly need can be easily found online,

Left: "United we are strong, United we will win." 1943 American WWII poster showing cannons, each with the flag of an Allied nation, blasting into the sky.

Members of the Armenian community hold Armenian flags and placards during a demonstration on April 24, 2015 in front of the Turkish consulate in Jerusalem.

that propaganda can be easily spotted, and that misinformation will be readily exposed for what it is. But propaganda can be subtle, and even patent manipulation can go undetected if it is on par with what audiences already think they know. Modern advertising uses many of the same techniques and it works even when the consumer knows all the tricks already. One has only to look at modern political campaigns to see propaganda in action.

Social media, like print and radio before it, can be employed to promote causes and spread ideas. Like any other medium social media is a natural tool for both evil and worthy purposes.

iHUMAN

THE EVOLUTION OF THE E-GO

I t wasn't long ago when most Americans didn't even access to a personal computer. Nowadays, most young adults in the West cannot even conceive of a world without personal electronic devices. We carry them in our pockets, and soon we'll even be wearing them—if devices such as Apple's iWatch take off.

The time when we implant technology directly into our bodies and have homes with appliances, lights, and door locks all connected to each other and managed online is just around the corner. The ubiquity of social media, which accustoms us to being constantly connected, is likely the beginning of something much more all-encompassing.

FACEBOOK

Facebook started in February 2004, when Mark Zuckerberg created a website called TheFacebook.com, expanding on earlier work he had done with a student-only program called FaceMash. TheFacebook.com allowed users—restricted at the time to Harvard students—to create a personal profile and make connections with one another. It became enormously popular on the Harvard campus and eventually opened up to most universities in North America. In 2005 the company became Facebook, and by September 2006 any person over the age of 13 who had an email address could sign up.

Facebook has evolved and expanded, allowing companies and individuals to create pages for their businesses that are connected to, but separate from, their profiles. Paid advertising was added, first in the form of sidebar ads, and later as timeline posts that looked almost exactly like posts for things the user had "liked." Facebook's changes over the years have often irritated users, but the number of registered members has continued to grow exponentially. Some people love to hate Facebook, but most keep using it as their main way of staying in touch with others.

TWITTER

Twitter launched in March 2006 as a social network that only allowed status updates ("tweets") of 140 characters at a time. 'Microblogging', as this way of broadcasting is called, was initially met with hesitation, but it quickly became popular. The service requires considerably less time from its user, providing an easy way to keep up with people.

The main feature of Twitter is its short 140 characters-long tweets, but it also allows direct messages between users and the ability to alert users to a tweet by including their Twitter handle prefixed by the "@" symbol. Similarly, hashtags (words or phrases without spaces, prefixed by the "#" symbol) act as metadata, allowing users to search for tagged tweets.

Initially free of advertising—though users could, and did, post tweets that were essentially ads—Twitter later added "promoted tweets" that inserted paid ads into users' feeds, much like Facebook places ads in users' timelines.

As the two biggest social networks, Facebook and Twitter compete for user numbers and advertising dollars, but are distinct enough that many people use both. Facebook works best for reconnecting with old friends and acquaintances and keeping up with family members—which may explain why it has attracted an older demographic.

Twitter, on the other hand, is best suited for as-it's-happening updates, and although each tweet is restricted in length, it has not prevented users from engaging in lengthy discussions in real time. Founded as a social media site, Twitter has become a go-to news source for millions of users.

I, CYBORG

At first, social media sites required logging in and out and spending time scrolling through feeds and timelines to see what had happened since the last login. Eventually, the growing use of mobile devices meant that all reputable and popular social media platforms developed mobile apps for users "on the go." Apps use notifications that notify users in real time. Constantly being connected is now both possible and common—not to mention addictive.

Our relationship with technology is changing, as new academic fields like Technoself Studies and Digital Humanities show. The focus of technoself studies is not just technology, but the shifts in our perception and understanding of the self in relation to it. There may come a day when human identity is so intertwined with technology that the two are inseparable. People are already exposing so much of their inner self on the Internet, that the idea doesn't seem so far-fetched. Identities are constructed and obscured on social media at such a degree that the questions of authenticity and the relation of the avatar to the IRL (In Real Life) person are already fascinating and inspiring sociologists and anthropologists.

Exponential advances in technology may soon bring about a kind of artificial intelligence that we can neither comprehend nor control. That moment, known as "the singularity," may indeed be way closer than we expect.

BUYING INFLUENCE

SHARING YOURSELF, OR SELLING YOUR LIFE TO THE HIGHEST BIDDER?

One of the most common complaints people voice about Facebook and Twitter is the presence of ads—not so much the sidebar ads, which are concentrated on one side and are easy to ignore, but those that are integrated within the user's timeline or feed and look exactly like posts by friends (until you look closely and notice the discreet identifying label). Yet few people would choose to pay for an ad-free site.

Businesses have come to realize the infinite potential of social media as advertising platforms—and the social media companies have been equally quick to satisfy that demand. In the end, it's all about social dynamics: Even though the various groups on social media are virtual, their behavior resembles that of real-world groups. "Groupthink" applies, although the actual outcome of this collective deliberation depends highly on the group's particular makeup and degree of homogeneity.

Like-minded groups are easier for advertisers to sell to: Once advertisers identify one person interested in the content of the ad, they can safely assume that the entire group will be reasonably interested as well. On the other hand, a group made up of dissimilar individuals makes the sell harder, as the chances of disagreement and uncertainty are higher.

AD-FREE, FOR A PRICE

Social media companies know these facts. They know social media have the potential to amplify the impact of advertising, but they're also aware of users' disfavor of blatant promotion. The answer for many companies has been to build paywalls, separating free from paid-for: either a free site infested with ads, or a premium one without. DeviantArt, for example, offers both free and premium versions of its site, but no advertising is not the only perk paying users get: they also get more features, like customizable profile skins.

Some sites that tried a premium ad-free model came to realize that users simply don't see enough benefit to opt for the paid-for experience. In other instances, developers ended up concentrating so much on the premium version that free users saw no value in the service and ended up leaving the site altogether. A perfect example of the former is Ning, a site that provided users with tools to create their own social networks. In the beginning, people flocked to Ning for its niche interest groups, and the ability it gave users to hold multiple memberships from a single account. But soon after Ning decided to remove its free option entirely, requiring those small groups to enforce membership fees. That drove many of Ning's users away and in search of other providers. Though Ning offered more to paid users than just an ad-free environment the model didn't work as well as it did for DeviantArt, and today few people have heard of Ning.

One solution to the advertising conundrum has been to create ads that are so obvious users can easily ignore them. Of course, that poses the danger of alienating users because of its intrusiveness, or render the ad so obvious it becomes practically worthless. DeviantArt's free version features content that is obviously promotional, but because the site is art-oriented, the ads are carefully curated to appeal to that specific crowd.

GOING INCOGNITO, GOING VIRAL

Facebook is an industry leader when it comes to advertising. The world's largest social media site is also the world's largest collector of personal information, which is then used to tailor and target advertising. Sometimes the results are amusing, and many Facebook users enjoy poking fun at how irrelevant some ads that appear on their pages are. But when this system works it works well, and it can induce users to voluntarily visit and end up following companies whose ads have appeared in their timelines.

Now businesses want to go beyond just serving ads that appeal to individual users. Most people place way more weight on the opinion and recommendations of personal friends than

{ **Suspected sock-puppet reviews** became a popular topic on the Kindle Boards (kboards), a forum for both Kindle authors and readers. }

DID YOU KNOW

Google for a long time offered "sponsored links" as the only advertising option. Advertisers could bid on keywords, and whenever a search containing those keywords was performed, the relevant ads would be served alongside search results. Making sponsored links both distinct from actual content, and similar enough that they may accidentally be selected, proved to be a great challenge for Google.

on the obvious promotional efforts of a company. Advertisers have quickly responded to that by designing ads that look like personal endorsements rather than generic marketing.

Twitter's ads, for example, take the form of "promoted" tweets. These tweets usually come from large corporations, but the feature itself is available to anyone who can pay the advertising fees, giving up-and-coming artists, comedians, and writers an opportunity to reach mass audiences.

Another way advertisers capitalize on friends' recommendations is by making posts go viral—images, videos, and catchy slogans so appealing that millions of users share them. Friends and family see them, enjoy them, and pass them on. It seems impossible to predict which image or post will end up becoming viral, let alone give it the degree of popularity that would make it a trend, but many marketers have cracked the code and turned viral advertising into a science.

FAKE FOLLOWERS AND SOCK PUPPETS

Businesses and individuals promoting their work online will be told by books and websites that they should aim to attract followers on social media because a popular post is unrivaled in creating brand recognition.

This idea has become so established in modern self-promotion lore that companies have sprung up offering "likes" and "follows" for a fee. The fact that these likes and follows will actually be from bots and sock-puppet accounts (that is, accounts that don't have actual people behind them, or that have one person running many accounts simply for the purpose of selling likes and follows) seems irrelevant; although a person or company interested in spending money on obtaining followers will likely serve themselves better by creating more engaging, interesting content or developing a more robust social media strategy. There are seemingly endless online posts and videos about how to create shareable, likable, potentially viral content.

THE RUSSIAN ZUCKERBERG

RUSSIA IS "INCOMPATIBLE WITH INTERNET BUSINESS" FOR ONE ENTREPRENEUR

Pavel Durov is a businessman who became known as the "Mark Zuckerberg of Russia" when he founded a popular social media site in his home country. Durov earned a first-class degree in philology from Saint Petersburg State University and just after graduating he founded the social network VKontakte.com (later known simply as VK), inspired by Facebook.

VK became Russia's most popular social network, with 100 million users, but, predictably, it got Durov into trouble with the Russian government. When asked to hand over information about certain Ukrainian protesters in April 2014, Durov refused. Later that month he was ousted as chief executive, leading many to speculate that Putin's government orchestrated.

The same year, Durov left Russia and cofounded a new company, Digital Fortress, whose first product is a largely open-source, instant-messaging app called Telegram. The specific appeal of Telegram is that it features secure encryption and self-destructing messages (including photos, videos, and other files). Durov has also wisely chosen the locations for his app's servers so as to avoid legal pressure for revealing users' details.

WHO'S WATCHING WHOM?

THE ART OF CASUAL SURVEILLANCE

Millions of people join social media sites to keep in touch with family and friends who live far away. Others join just to share what they do and where they go. Posting glimpses of a great restaurant or a memorable performance is a fun way to share your life with friends. But your friends aren't the only ones watching.

CHECK IN, GET CHECKED OUT

After the launch of Foursqaure, an app that lets users share their location, "checking in" became a routine feature of social media. Foursquare can be linked to other social media accounts so a user's check-ins also appear in real time on Twitter, Facebook, and other sites. Foursquare's instant success led other apps and sites to add the check in capability as well, making it such an ordinary feature of online life that few thought of its side effects.

Location data didn't begin with Foursquare, of course. Digital camera manufacturers have been providing consumers with a way to stamp location metadata to photographs for years, primarily so that users can have a record of where vacation snapshots were taken. At first, users had to add the data manually after downloading the images to a computer; once provided, the information stayed with the image along with technical information, like aperture, shutter speed, and type of camera.

Most smartphones now have Global Positioning System (GPS) capability, along with Wi-Fi (which can also be used in location tracking), and camera phones add location data to images unless it is manually turned off. Location services are used not only by the phone's camera, but also by its mapping software, and can be activated for a variety of other apps—it's essentially the same information that Foursquare uses to allow people to check in.

BIG BROTHER

Smartphone owners tend to think of location services as a convenience: a nifty feature that tags photographs with the location they were shot, points their location on a map, and could help retrieve misplaced phones. But this information isn't accessible only to the rightful owner of said device.

Both Apple and Google, and possibly other smartphone and software makers, have software in place that stores information about where phones—and their users—have been. Whenever a user makes a backup on their computer, or updates firmware, that information is transmitted to the maker. Apple and Google are both eager to collect, store and analyze a variety of data about their users, supposedly in order to better serve them.

Many governments would welcome the opportunity to legally gather their citizens' phone data. In a world plagued by the ominous threat of terrorist attacks, protecting individual privacy can be superseded by the need to protect civilians, an argument commonly advanced today, in spite of Benjamin Franklin's insightful aphorism that "those who sacrifice liberty for security deserve neither." It is a well-known fact that government agencies collect and store emails, phone data, and other personal information—even if nothing is ever done with most of it.

> *It is a well-known fact that government agencies collect and store emails, phone data, and other personal information.*

Nevertheless, several government agencies, the FBI and Department of Homeland Security among them, are actively developing the technology to gather information from social media. Whether these activities are legal is another question. Both the American Civil Liberties Union (ACLU) and Canadian Civil Liberties Association (CCLA) have been monitoring attempts by their respective governments to pass laws sanctioning large-scale surveillance.

PATRIOTS, ALL

The USA PATRIOT Act (commonly known as the Patriot Act) was passed by Congress shortly after the September 11, 2001,

terrorist attacks. It is an intricate piece of legislation heavily criticized for the considerable access to personal information, records, and physical property it provides law enforcement agencies.

In addition to that, the Patriot Act allows law enforcement to collect said information without either knowledge or the consent of the person under surveillance. In fact, the Patriot Act is designed to apply to any individual, whether charged or not.

At the time the law was passed, it wasn't met with any opposition from lawmakers. The 9/11 events showed America's vulnerability to terrorism. Any law that would facilitate the job of the various agencies seemed at the time both reasonable and necessary. But in the years since 2001, the act has suffered severe criticism from groups, such as the ACLU, on account of the high risk of infringing on privacy.

PASSING THE CENSORS

Like propaganda, information can also be used for good or ill. Governments insist that they only use the information they gather for the protection of their citizens but the same information could very well be used to control them—unless the citizens claim back control of their own data.

A WWI propaganda poster depicting Kaiser Wilhelm II as a spider at the center of an invisible web, c. 1918.

Governments and lawmakers also argue that certain information must remain confidential. The phrase "loose lips sink ships" was a catchy saying during wartime to make people think twice about the information they were parting with and to whom. Information that threatens national security should be kept secret. The problem persists: Who decides what should be public knowledge, and what should be kept secret?

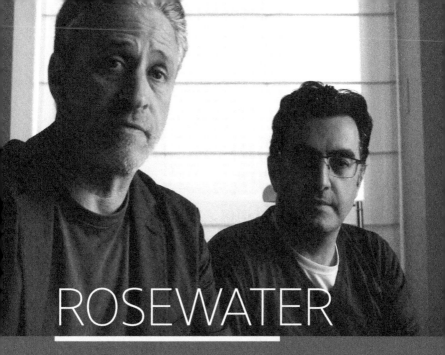

ROSEWATER

IN 2009 Iranian-Canadian journalist Maziar Bahari appeared on the satirical comedy news program *The Daily Show*, where he was interviewed by host Jon Stewart. Later, Bahari was arrested by Iranian authorities and imprisoned for 118 days—he was blindfolded, tortured, and interrogated under suspicion of spying for the US government.

After his release, Bahari wrote a book about his experiences that was made into a movie starring Gael García Bernal. Jon Stewart, whose show was used as evidence in Bahari's arrest, took on the roles of screenwriter and director for the film, in a departure into serious journalism. *Rosewater* won the Freedom of Expression Award from the US National Board of Review in 2014; it was also nominated for a Phoenix Film Critics Society Award.

THE TOP 10

SHARE

SOCIAL MEDIA PLATFORMS

1. **Facebook** With an estimated 900 million unique monthly users, Facebook is top not only in its home country of America, but everywhere in the world.

2. **Twitter** Not surprisingly, the United States' second-biggest social media platform, Twitter, is the world's too, with 310 million unique monthly users.

3. **LinkedIn** More professional networking-focused, LinkedIn boasts 255 million unique monthly users.

4. **Pinterest** Users "pin" images, websites, and other online content onto virtual boards that they can share with other users. It has grown from modest beginnings to 250 million unique monthly visitors.

5 Google Plus Many social media fans joke about how G+ is one of Google's mammoth failures—it was intended to take on and decimate Facebook as the top social platform, after all. But with 120 million unique monthly visitors and fifth place worldwide, it can't exactly be called a "failure."

6 Tumblr A blogging platform that makes it extremely easy to share and "reblog" other users' posts, Tumblr has amassed 110 million unique monthly visitors.

7 Instagram The top image-sharing social media app, Instagram doesn't do much beyond allow users to post pictures and short videos—but it does it very, very well. Every month 100 million unique users post, like, and comment on photos. In 2012, Facebook acquired Instagram for $1 billion.

8 VK At 80 million unique monthly users, VK is Russia's top social media platform and eighth in the world (see page 30 for more about its founder).

9 Flickr Once a popular image-hosting website, Flickr also developed a mobile app, and now has 65 million unique monthly users. Flickr is owned by Yahoo.

10 Vine Owned by Twitter, Vine has 42 million unique monthly users, who post six-second videos.

GOVERNMENT INFILTRATION OF ACTIVIST GROUPS

COUNTERINTELLIGENCE AGAINST DOMESTIC TERRORISM OR HOLDING THE PARTY LINE?

Governments around the world, and the US government in particular, have long histories of infiltrating groups that plot to work against them, especially when those groups are inside their own borders. While the primary purpose of a government is governing, it also needs to maintain its monopoly on power. Any group that advocates change, even if it's for the common good, can be classified as a threat.

The purpose of infiltrating activist groups is double: the first is to find out what the groups are up to. People will reveal more to those they believe to be on the same side or working toward the same goal as them, so installing government agents into an

Above: WikiLeaks supporters hold pictures in support of WikiLeaks founder Julian Assange. Madrid, December 11, 2010.

activist group can yield inside information that could be proven useful. Second, infiltrating activist groups can thwart the group's efforts if its activities are perceived as a threat. Spreading misinformation and protecting the government's status quo can be much more effective when the source is a trusted member of the group.

After activists moved their organizations online, and especially on social media, governments quickly followed suit. The anonymity that the web provides both helps and hinders counterintelligence. It makes it easier for government agents to remain covert, but it also makes it harder to identify those behind activity governments might consider threatening.

COINTELPRO

Although governmental infiltration is part and parcel of ruling regimes, it was FBI-orchestrated COINTELPRO in the 1970s that confirmed everyone's worst fears.

At its inception, COINTELPRO's main target was the United States Communist Party, although it also targeted a range of other groups and individuals, including the Civil Rights Movement, the American Indian Movement, the women's rights movement, the Ku Klux Klan, groups protesting the Vietnam War, and many others. Although some groups may have posed actual threats to national security, others were seen merely as "subversive."

The tactics that were employed by the FBI during that operation are typical of those still used today to penetrate and disrupt activist movements, and while most of those are technically

{ **COINTELPRO** stands for COunter INTELligence PROgram, and ran from 1956 to 1971, when it was officially dissolved. Many of the tactics used in COINTELPRO have persisted, however. }

legal, others were less so. Infiltrators of "subversive" groups work to create a negative public image by releasing carefully selected, sometimes doctored, personal information about he group members, and the infiltrators work hard to create a sentiment of distrust amongst group members.

OPERATION BACKFIRE

Common targets for infiltration have included groups that are active in animal rights and environmental causes. Some radical organizations have resorted to violence to reach their desired goals, but very few environmental groups present an active terrorism threat.

In 2004 the FBI formed Operation Backfire, grouping together a number of separate investigations into animal rights and environmental groups. The goal of the operation was to investigate domestic terrorism, and the primary targets were the Earth Liberation Front (ELF) and the Animal Liberation Front (ALF).

In all, 18 activists were indicted for acts of eco-terrorism, but the arrests drew criticism from the National Lawyers Guild and others. Some of the accused, it is claimed, were not even members of

Outside the Bloomington, Indiana police headquarters environmental activists protest the arrests of several critical mass riders and an activist accused of tree spiking.

the ELF or the ALF, but peaceful activists who would have never engaged in terrorism.

Social media platforms have become an efficient way for activists to organize—both peaceful, nonviolent groups and terrorist organizations use social media. In order to conduct surveillance, the FBI and other agencies are now monitoring social media.

THE APPS

Facebook and Twitter allow users to post images as well as text updates, links, and other information, but some social media apps focus almost exclusively on image- and video-sharing. Here are some of the most popular.

INSTAGRAM (instagram.com)

Instagram is the best known of the photo-sharing apps. It can access a mobile device's camera directly and apply filters and image corrections right in the app, making it simple to snap and share images. It also allows sharing short videos.

VINE (VINE.CO)

Twitter was originally best suited for text and, to share images, users had to link to an outside site. Later on, Twitter added in-app viewing of images and videos and the social media company also bought Vine, an app for recording and sharing video clips. Though Twitter and Vine remain separate apps, they are linked so that Vines can appear within Twitter.

SNAPCHAT (SNAPCHAT.COM)

Instagram and Twitter/Vine are largely public platforms for sharing images (although both can be set up to keep content private). Snapchat filled a need for a predominantly off-the-record image-sharing app which allows users to send snapshots directly to others rather than posting them on a profile or feed. Images are deleted after viewing, keeping the communication secret.

YOUTUBE (YOUTUBE.COM)

Though not always a social media app, the immense video-sharing site YouTube has social media features, like the ability to set up one's own "channel," to follow others, make comments, "like" videos, and so on. It also has a stripped-down mobile app that includes most of the social media aspects of the site.

FLICKR (FLICKR.COM)

Created as an image-sharing website aimed primarily at photography buffs, Flickr was embraced by those looking for an easy way to share images of all kinds. To remain competitive, Flickr later developed an app as well, making it easier for users to share images, follow other users, and create thematic groups.

500PX (500PX.COM)

As Flickr expanded to many types of images, 500px remained solidly committed to serious photography. The site and its companion app allow photographers to post images, follow other users, and promote their own and others' photographs.

THE ARAB
SPRING AND
THE ENSUING
WINTER

REVOLUTION IN REAL TIME

When used as a tool for spreading information organizing activists, and selling products and ideas, social media has immense potential. But it was not really apparent how great that potential was until a series of uprisings in the Middle East demonstrated just what Facebook and Twitter could do to change the world.

In late 2010 and early 2011, the general unrest in several Middle Eastern countries—including countries that had seemed relatively stable—erupted into protests, revolutions, and coups. The series of events that unfolded over the following months became known as "the Arab Spring." And, although the use of social media was

Left: A Muslim supporter of the Islamist Ennahda party during an election rally in Tunisia.

different in kind from previous uses of traditional media, its reach was exponentially greater.

IT BEGINS IN TUNISIA

The Arab Spring's origins can be traced back to December 2010, when a street vendor finally reached the end of his tether with the bureaucracy and police abuse that left him incapable of making a decent living. Mohamed Bouazizi set himself on fire in protest, igniting not only his own flesh, but the passions of his fellow Tunisians.

Tunisia had seemed politically stable, at least compared to its volatile neighbors, and was touted as a pleasant tourist destination for Westerners. Many people were therefore surprised read in their Twitter feeds that it had become the stage of violent protests against government corruption and police brutality. Tunisia's armed forces refused to suppress the protests, and about a month after Bouazizi's self-immolation, President Zine el-Abidine Ben Ali was forced to flee the country.

In January 2011, Tunisia found itself in a state of political transition. A new government was elected in October that year, but disputes over the new constitution and lack of improvement to living conditions for the Tunisian people kept the situation flammable. Unrest persisted as the new government—a parliamentary democracy dominated by Islamists in coalition with secular parties—tried to negotiate religion's role in the new Tunisia. Negotiations and intermittent protest are ongoing as the struggle for a stable Tunisia continues. In December 2014, Tunisia held its first free presidential election since the events of the Arab Spring. How new president Beji Caid Essebi will manage the push for further democratic reform and the threats from militant Islamist groups remains to be seen.

THE FALL OF MUBARAK

The Arab Spring may have begun in Tunisia, but what had a profound effect on Westerners was the way it spread to Egypt. Egypt was the West's biggest ally in the Middle East, so the downfall of President Hosni Mubarak came as a shock.

In power since 1981, Mubarak's government had gradually become less effective and indifferent to the hardship and widespread unemployment of his people. Mubarak's tolerance of a free press, ironically, had a great deal to do with his own downfall. Both the institutional press and the people's press (social media) broadcast to the world events as they were unfolding, including the occupation of Tahrir Square in Cairo. On February 11, 2011, when the Egyptian military refused to suppress the occupation, President Mubarak was forced to step down.

The fall of Egypt's president left the military in power, and deep divisions in political ideology meant protests continued and the economy declined rapidly. An Islamist party won the parliamentary elections, but its relationship with secular parties was tense, leaving the country in perpetual turmoil. In July 2013, further widespread protests forced the Egyptian military to remove the elected president and prepare for a new election. It has been, and continues to be, a difficult transition from a formerly autocratic rule to a version of a liberal democracy.

SOCIAL MEDIA AND GEZI PARK

In December 2012, Turkish residents opposing construction in Gezi Park, one of the only green spaces in Istanbul, signed a petition in protest. The petition didn't yield any measurable outcome, so in May 2013, people began gathering in the park, camping

Libya confilct, 2011.

out in a peaceful sit-in. The Turkish government responded by raiding the encampment, galvanizing outrage throughout the country and starting a series of protests, encampments, and sit-ins, all of which met with tear gas, water cannons, and arrests.

What was different about the Gezi Park protests was not the clash of citizens and police, or the way social media was used to organize and mobilize protestors, but the extent to which people around the world became aware of events. Although social media had been used before in organizing protesters, this was the first time that nearly everyone with a Twitter account knew what was going on as it was happening.

Information, images, and videos of the protests spread instantly, confirming the power of social media to keep people dynamically informed. Since then, real-time information about far-off events has become the new normal—and it exists in the social media.

EUROPEAN UNION AND UKRAINE

More than 100,000 people—many of them students—gathered in Kiev's Independence Square in early December 2013, defying a ban on protests in the city's center. They gathered to express their anger against Ukrainian President Viktor Yanukovych's refusal to sign a trade agreement with the European Union, a move that would have brought Ukraine one step closer to joining the EU, and would have resulted in greater independence from Russia.

Further clashes between protesters and police, as citizens clamored for political change, resulted in President Yanukovych fleeing Kiev. Not long afterward, Russian President Vladimir Putin annexed the entire Crimean peninsula, claiming that 97 percent of its people had voted to join Russia. Western powers objected that the referendum was a sham and refused to support Putin's move.

In June 2014, what remained of Ukraine under newly elected President Petro Poroshenko signed the deal with the European Union that Yanukovych had turned down. The European Union also agreed to impose economic sanctions on Russia and a peace deal was signed, but it was soon violated by pro-Russian rebels. As of March 2015, repeated attempts at peace talks and cease-fires continued to remain fruitless.

In what looked to Western eyes like a domino effect, but was, in fact, far more complicated and nuanced in the countries involved, protests and political shifts followed throughout the Middle East. In Libya, protests against Muammar al-Qaddafi's authoritarian regime broke out in February 2011 but instead of a quick change of regime followed by a long period of transition, the protests escalated into civil war. Even the intervention of NATO forces on behalf of the rebels—which led to Qaddafi's assassination in October 2011—was short-lived. Various rebel

IN A GALAXY...

Tunisian public relations' claims about the country's tourist potential are not merely propaganda, at least for a certain part of the Western world. George Lucas's beloved film Star Wars was filmed in the Tunisian Sahara desert, and many vestiges of the film—including parts of a huge fake skeleton and the real Tunisian villages that stood in for Tatooine—are popular destinations for Star Wars fans.

groups divided up the country, and the new central government, although composed of a secular political alliance elected by the people, was too weak to inspire consensus.

Syria, ruled by an oppressive regime headed by President Bashar al-Assad, has been a key political ally of Iran. Being a multireligious country in a region infested with never-ending religious clashes, there was little doubt that the political unrest of the Arab Spring would affect Syria. Unlike what happened in many nearby countries, Syria's troubles did not start in major urban areas. Syrian protests began in provincial towns, then spread to larger cities.

Though Syria has a variety of religions, the majority of its people follow the Sunni sect of Islam, while the president and his government mostly belong to the Alawite minority, which has not helped to temper dissent. In addition, the Syrian government has the support of both Iran and Russia, while the rebels are supported by Saudi Arabia. These differences have resulted in a protracted and bloody civil war.

Other Middle Eastern countries were affected by the Arab Spring on a smaller scale. Bahrain saw protests by the largely Shiite Muslim populace against the royal family who are Sunni Muslims. The military intervention of Saudi Arabia and other neighboring countries saved the royal family but did not entirely suppress dissent.

Morocco and Jordan fared better, despite widespread protests in early 2011 demanding improved living conditions, limits on the power of the two countries' royal families, and an end to governmental corruption. Morocco's King Mohammed VI willingly gave up some of his power and agreed to constitutional amendments, while Jordan's King Abdullah II made changes in his government to forestall the chaos other countries had suffered. The people of both countries preferred to reform their current systems rather than abolish their monarchies; rallies and protests continue, however, indicating that change is not yet complete.

MARTIAL LAW IN THAILAND

In May 2014, Thailand's military seized control of the government, suspending the constitution and imposing martial law. The reason, the story went, was to restore order and bring about political reform, though it is hard to see how suspending the country's constitution would help the citizens.

There had been widespread political unrest for some time before the military took control; although the government was

Al-Qaeda and the Islamic State of Iraq and Syria (aka ISIS) are often lumped together as the same extremist Islamic group that seeks to return the Middle East (or large parts of it) to strict religious rule. In fact, although ISIS grew out of al-Qaeda— it was formerly a branch of al-Qaeda in Iraq—the two groups now compete for followers and territory. ISIS is very skilled in its use of social media to recruit followers and intimidate opponents—especially those in Western countries.

democratically elected, dissidents claimed there was so much corruption that a new government was in order. Violence ensued between pro- and anti-government factions—which were largely made up of urban middle class and poor rural people respectively—prompting the military to take over and impose a curfew and a ban on public gatherings of more than five people.

As oppressive regimes are known to do, the military ordered all broadcasters to cease regular programming, knowing that whoever controls the flow of information has the upper hand. But information is uncontainable, and the one thing Thais on both sides of the political spectrum wonder is why King Bhumibol hasn't stepped in to end the conflict. Although the king is a constitutional monarch, he was—until very recently—respected and loved across the political divide.

One thing that is patently different about conflict in the 21st century is that it is observed by the whole world. It is no more just heroic war correspondents following armies, but also citizens often armed with nothing more than their cell phones who break news.

Social media may have begun as a primarily Western phenomenon, but it has spread worldwide. In the six months following Egypt's revolution, Facebook users in that country soared from 450,000 to 3 million. By July 2013 there were 5 million Egyptians on Facebook. In parts of the world where there is political unrest, the tweets and status updates of everyday citizens will keep the rest of the world on its toes.

CATCH AND RELEASE

O ne of Sony Pictures' planned releases for 2014 was *The Interview*, a comedy about a plot to assassinate North Korean leader Kim Jong-un, starring Seth Rogen and James Franco. A North Korean spokesman promised retaliation if the movie was released, but no one took the threat seriously. On November 22, several Sony Pictures employees arrived at work to find their computer system was malfunctioning. The incident was initially brushed off as a regular IT problem, but it was soon revealed that Sony had been hacked by a group calling itself GOP, or "Guardians of Peace"—possibly a North Korean group aided by former Sony employees.

GOP tried to halt the release of the movie by threatening to reveal secret information stolen from Sony Pictures' servers. When Sony ignored the threat, the group put several unreleased movies online, where they were downloaded countless times before they had even hit theaters. Then GOP leaked private emails from several Sony employees, and social media helped make damning excerpts from those emails go viral. Sony pulled *The Interview*, but eventually went ahead with it as a scaled-back release.

MEET
YOUR MEDIA

THE BIRTH OF
CITIZEN JOURNALISM

For as long as home video equipment has been around, viewers have contributed footage to television news. This has especially been the case for local news, where the everyday experiences of people become newsworthy items. Those amateur videos and photographs were a standard form that kept viewers and readers interested. Nowadays, citizen journalism is noticeably more common, and viewers looking for news can bypass traditional media altogether.

Although global news organizations have reporters and journalists on the scene very quickly, it's often only the people in the thick of it that know exactly what is happening and what is about to happen. While news media conglomerates write stories that provide context to events, the people actually involved are much better suited to tell the story of what it is like to be part of them.

People in North America and Europe could browse their Twitter feeds and Instagram accounts to view images and videos and read updates from Turkish protesters in Gezi Park. They were able to access firsthand accounts of the protesters' arrests in Kiev's Independence Square, or browse images of military brutality in Thailand moments after it occurred.

Big news organizations can, and do, show some of the same information. *The Telegraph*, for example, had reporters onsite when the Kiev protests began. But in many countries experiencing widespread social and political unrest, local and foreign news media are under government control. Reports of what is happening in Thailand, for example—where not only are the state media controlled, but also regular broadcasts have been shut down—may be filtered and doctored accordingly by the

Left: A protester wearing an Anonymous mask records the Anonymous Million Mask March in Portland on her cell phone.

government. Faced with state-controlled media, people on the streets armed with a cell-phone camera and a data plan provide an alternative to the official account viewpoint.

Contemporary news programs commonly include Twitter feeds, Facebook posts, and YouTube videos as part of their coverage of everything from local sports events to political unrest. Traditional news outlets have had a hard time remaining relevant and have started including social media in their regular reportage, and recruiting viewers to upload and share videos, sometimes cobbling together entire stories from Twitter using trending hashtags.

VIRTUAL VIRALITY

WHAT MAKES A VIDEO GO VIRAL?

Every advertiser and politician wants their posts to go viral (unless they're the damaging kind) but few can agree exactly what that entails. When someone says a video or a tweet has "gone viral," it means the post has garnered a large number of views, shares, and re-posts in a short period. How many views and how short a period are debated notions.

Popular YouTuber Kevin Nalty said in 2011 that only a few years back a video could be considered viral if it got a million views, but suggested that 5 million views in a week or less was a more realistic definition.

If a video or other post makes it really big, other video makers and social media users will try to emulate it. Some will make their own versions to cash in on the hype, while others will make parodies that become viral in their own right. And while viral phenomena are usually short-lived, staying in the collective consciousness for a only few weeks or months, other will be remembered for much longer.

THE LISTICLE-IFICATION

MORE INFORMATION, LESS ENGAGEMENT?

Fewer people are reading long-form journalism, and instead prefer scanning headlines, looking at top-10 lists, and watching short videos before moving on to the next thing. In a somewhat ironic sign of the times, an internal *New York Times* report leaked to Buzzfeed in May 2014 highlighted the dismal state of digital media for traditional institutions. The *Times* report revealed, "Huffington Post surpassed us years ago in reader traffic and BuzzFeed pulled ahead in 2013." Popular sites like Huffington Post and BuzzFeed, known for its lists and pithy summaries

Above: Arianna Huffington, founder of news website The Huffington Post, speaks during a session at the annual meeting of the World Economic Forum (WEF) in Davos, January 24, 2014.

derived from content that originally appeared elsewhere, capitalize on short attention spans. Even news sites that feature more in-depth coverage include plenty of short pieces, lists, and clickbait articles to keep viewers from leaving the site too quickly.

This is considered a negative development, but there is another side to it. With such an abundance of content from around the world readily available, the only way to stay ahead of the game is to reduce and condense content to the absolute essentials. For those that have both the time and the inclination, long-form articles are still very much in existence, and they are even gaining popularity. Websites like the blogging platform Medium's spin-off online magazine *Matter* contain almost entirely long, considered articles on a variety of topics, and links to those articles are frequently shared on social media.

Readers' attention spans have become shorter since the onset of online journalism, but that may be a result of how information is shared—and not a declining function of the human brain. If the availability of apps like Pocket (with 17 million users and 1 billion items saved for offline reading) and the "reading list" built into Apple's Safari browser are any indication, people browse quickly, check headlines and scan lists, but save longer articles to read offline, when they're relaxing at home, and have more time to unwind and think.

Social media facilitates both kinds of reading. Quick reads for short attention spans are shared the most, but longer reads get around, too. Truly good writing will be shared over and over, while superficial memes and silly lists tend to spike in popularity and then quickly fade into obscurity. They may pop up again at some point, and the nature of the Internet means they will never go away entirely. These listicles are like icicles—cool for a while, but then they vanish.

PLUS ONE(S)

TWITTER AND FACEBOOK ACQUISITIONS

Twitter has been steadily building its flock since 2008 by buying up other social media software companies and digital service providers. Here is a timeline of Twitter's noteworthy acquisitions in recent years.

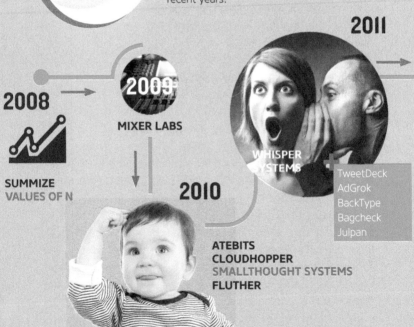

2011

2008

SUMMIZE
VALUES OF N

2009

MIXER LABS

2010

ATEBITS
CLOUDHOPPER
SMALLTHOUGHT SYSTEMS
FLUTHER

WHISPER SYSTEMS

TweetDeck
AdGrok
BackType
Bagcheck
Julpan

2012

SUMMIFY
DASIENT
POSTEROUS
HOTSPOTS.IO
RESTENGINE
NCLUD
VINE
CABANA

2014

GNIP
NAMO MEDIA
TAPCOMMERCE
CARDSPRING
MITRO

2015

ZIPDIAL

LUCKY
SORT

2013

Crashlytics
Ubalo
Spindle Labs
Locomatix
Marakana
Trendrr
MoPub

BLUEFIN
LABS

YES!

Facebook has added a few friends since its inception in 2007. Year by year, the company has acquired a number of other tech ventures, including these.

2009
FRIENDFEED

2008
CONNECTU

2007

2013
ATLAS
OSMETA
HOT STUDIO
SPACEPORT.IO
PARSE
MONOIDICS
JIBBIGO
ONAVA
SPORTSTREAM

PARAKEY

2014
LITTLE EYE LABS

WAVEGROUP SOUND

+ Branch
WhatsApp
Oculus VR
Acenta
ProtoGeo OY
PrivateCore

http://www.friendster.

2010

OCTAZEN SOLUTIONS
DIVVYSHOT
FRIENDSTER
SHAREGROVE
NEXTSTOP
CHAI LABS
HOT POTATO
DROP.IO

2011

SOFA
+

Rel8tion
Beluga
Snaptu
RecRec
Daytum
MailRank
Push Pop Press
Friend.ly
Strobe
Gowalla

2012

INSTAGRAM
TAGTILE
GLANCEE
LIGHTBOX
KARMA
FACE.COM
SPOOL
ACRYLIC SOFTWARE
THREADSY

2015

YES!

WIT.AI
QUICKFIRE
THEFIND

#MOVEMENT

A BRIEF HISTORY
OF HASHTAGS

IN August 2007, open-source advocate Chris Messina suggested using the pound symbol as a way of organizing posts on Twitter. His original tweet about the idea proposed its use to organize groups, but once it was adopted, hashtags quickly became used for tagging topics. The idea was inspired by the use of ampersands and hashes in Internet Relay Chat, or IRC, a precursor to today's social media, for labeling groups and topics.

By July 2009, Twitter had officially adopted the hashtag, making all unspaced words and phrases prefixed by the hash sign hyperlinked; this made it possible to search for more tweets with the same tag simply by clicking on the link. By 2010, there was a "Trending Topics" section on the Twitter homepage to show the most popular tags.

Hashtags are used in a variety of ways to organize Twitter content and add information to individual tweets. At its simplest, a hashtag can be used to tag a post with its topic—#amwriting, for example, tags posts related to writers at work, while #FF refers to "Follow Friday," when users suggest other Twitter accounts that their followers might want to look at.

Some people use hashtags to add humor to their posts, or to share their current state of mind, add a location (not as common

#BlackLivesMatter protest in Berkeley, California at the corner of College Avenue and Ashby on Saturday, December 13, 2014.

since Twitter added location-based functions), or include other types of information. Examples of these sorts of tags are #sorrynotsorry, #feelingblue, and #ilovebacon.

Since hashtags were introduced in Twitter, they have spread to other social media platforms. Hashtags are now used for tagging subject matter in Instagram and Flickr, where they are especially useful since both apps are image-focused and images are notoriously difficult to search for. Although Facebook users once made fun of hashtags in their posts, they now accept them as an integrated function. They are still, however, not as popular there, perhaps

The biggest issue facing citizen journalists in countries with government-controlled media is getting their content out to the world. That is one reason many activist groups make it a priority to set up Wi-Fi, satellite Internet, or cell phone access. Once an uncensored connection is established, a simple hashtag can help readers everywhere instantaneously events as they unfold.

SIGN OF THE TIMES

The symbol used to mark a hashtag (#) is commonly called the "pound sign" or "number sign" in North America, but it is often called the "hash sign" or "hash mark" in other parts of the world. It was once called the "octothorpe." The name "hash mark" probably derives from "hatch mark," in the sense of "hatching" or "cross-hatching," which is a type of mark used in art to create shading on a black-and-white drawing.

because Facebook works differently—and caters to a different audience.

Although Twitter, Instagram, and other social media platforms have embraced the hashtag, there is no official way to create a hashtag. Any user can add any hashtag to his or her posts (although some apps, like Twitter, monitor hashtag use and may suspend accounts that use hashtags inappropriately, and may even ban certain tags). Other users may then decide to adopt the same tag; if it becomes popular enough, it is trending.

The popularity of a hashtag can be the organic result of people coming across a tag and using it in their own posts. But hashtag creation can also be deliberate, as in the case of a group coming up with a tag to organize their activities and stay in touch, or inventing a memorable word to tag discussions online.

Social movements use social media to organize and inform, and hashtags are essential to their efforts. Sometimes a movement gives its name to the tag, and a tag may, conversely, give its name to a movement—making it difficult to tell which came first. Either way, the short phrase in a tag can define a movement. They're carefully chosen, often simple statements, that sum up the point of the movement, like #INeedFeminism or #BlackLivesMatter.

Some movements—not only create their own hashtags to organize like-minded people, but hijack popular tags that have nothing to do with them so that they can spread their message (or propaganda) as far as possible. ISIS, or the Islamic State, is particularly effective at hijacking hashtags. In several instances, it has had group members submit the most popular tags at the time, then use them to spread videos of executions of ISIS prisoners. The human infatuation with the obscene was enough to lead many people who wouldn't have knowingly pursued such material to ISIS videos, spreading the message much farther than it would have reached.

From a simple way to mark a sarcastic post (#sarcasm) to a means of organizing a local event (#VanCAF), to a tag that grows from a single protest to a national or international movement (#OccupyWallStreet), hashtags make the mass of information on social media more user-friendly. They are undoubtedly a powerful force for activism.

WE ARE THE
99%

OCCUPY

FROM WALL ST. TO THE WORLD

I n February 2011, the Canadian anticonsumerist publication
Adbusters proposed a march on Wall Street protesting the
influence of big corporations on government and banking, and
standing against income inequality. In July that year, they posted
a manifesto on their blog, using the hashtag #OccupyWallStreet
and showing an image of a dancer poised atop the famous Wall
Street *Charging Bull* statue. The post called for an occupation
of lower Manhattan on September 17. When the date arrived,
peaceful protesters flooded Zuccotti Park and set up camp. A
Facebook page was soon set up, and more and more people
began using the #OccupyWallStreet hashtag (later shortened
to #OWS) on Twitter.

Although organized by consensus discussions and without
appointed leaders, the Occupy Wall Street movement articulated
a list of grievances. OWS protesters generally wanted to see the

influence of corporations on politicians curbed, and they wanted the practices of banks monitored and regulated. The protesters wanted answers and aid for student debt, a solution to increasing unemployment, and a plan to address widening income inequality.

The slogan "We are the 99 percent" referred to the fact that in the United States 1 percent of the population sits on almost 25 percent of the entire wealth, and corporate CEOs earn more than 350 times the average worker's salary. Pew Research Center representative Paul Taylor called it "the most successful slogan since 'Hell no, we won't go,' which dates to the Vietnam era."

Although many of the issues raised by the OWS protesters remain unresolved years later, the movement was enormously successful in drawing attention to income inequality and the issues related to letting big business influence the political process. This success inspired protests in other areas as well, giving rise to a nationwide Occupy movement. New York City members called for a citywide strike, while other cities started their own Occupy demonstrations, organizing protests and other forms of civil disobedience.

OCCUPY BY VOTE

Occupy Wall Street had more structure than many realize. Each day, facilitators led high-level General Assembly meetings at Zuccotti Park. Smaller working groups were dedicated to hashing out specific issues, allowing anyone to propose an idea for discussion. Votes would be cast in the working groups, and any proposal that achieved a nine-tenths majority would be relayed to the General Assembly for bigger picture agenda-setting.

Occupy Wall Street protesters, Washington, DC, February 17, 2013

The movement, although no longer camped out in Manhattan, still fights to improve, or stall, income inequality. It has raised funds to buy out and forgive student loan debt, and campaigned for workers' rights. OWS inspired protesters across the world to self-organize, protest inequality, and demonstrate for similar causes.

Although the Occupy movement has been stressing the importance of peaceful protest, those involved have, since the beginning, been under surveillance by the FBI and the US Department of Homeland Security. Even peaceful movements have the potential to become violent, so keeping tabs on OWS protesters can be justified on the unfounded grounds of preventing domestic terrorism.

The extent to which the FBI has been monitoring events became clearer when people began using the United States' Freedom of Information Act to request FBI records relating to the movement. Not every request has been honored, and MIT doctoral student Ryan Shapiro has become famous for requesting large amounts of classified documents and suing the FBI for refusing requests on insufficient grounds. For example, when requesting information connected to an alleged assassination attempt on leaders of the Occupy Houston movement, Shapiro was given only five of the 17 pages identified as relevant—and all five were heavily redacted.

If the FBI is that invested in monitoring the Occupy movement, the implication is that the campaign had chances of becoming a vehicle for actual change.

The media, on the other hand, has generally been supportive of the Occupy movement. In 2011 instead of naming a prominent individual as "Person of the Year," *Time* gave the honor to "The Protester." The year 2011 was special in that regard, because new technologies and platforms sparked a cascade of protests across the globe, ushering in new movements for change. Choosing The Protester as Person of the Year highlights the power of social media—and the people using it—to do good.

HATERS, AN OVERVIEW

Social media has made group organization easier. It can facilitate activism, help plan social rallies, and turn attempts to manipulate public favor back on themselves. Social media can certainly be used for good but, like propaganda and other means of communication, social media is not itself good or bad—it is just a tool. Social media turns dangerous when it is used for ominous purposes, like bullying. The Internet troll is nearly as old as the Internet itself. Trolls are people who lurk on message boards, forums, and comment sections of websites, making comments intended to stir up trouble, offend, or anger users. In many cases, trolls genuinely stand their views and think that incessant harassment will help others see the truth. And sometimes—even *usually*—trolls just want to stir up trouble.

Social media turns dangerous when it is used for ominous purposes, like bullying.

Social media has facilitated "trolling" in the same way it has allowed other forms of communication. Trolls no longer need to lurk on forums, waiting for choice comments to reply to;

WAR ON WOMEN

Amanda Hess's "Why Women Aren't Welcome on the Internet," from the January *issue 2014 of* Pacific Standard, *painfully detailed her own experiences of getting death and rape threats— because of her online presence and writing. It also exposed how common this kind of harassment is and the lack of appropriate response by police.*

searching Twitter hashtags for favorite topics, they can either co-opt the tag for their own use, or find who is posting about what and spam their feed.

A favorite troll target is YouTube, where the comments tend to be especially nasty. This comes from the days when YouTube comments were still not moderated and could be left anonymously. Eventually, YouTube changed its commenting function, giving video creators more rights in managing comments, including blocking certain users. Viewers were also given more sorting options, so that the more relevant comments could appear at the top instead of being buried down the page. For a while, anonymous commenting was not allowed; it was effectively reinstated after eight months, because commenting requires a Google+ account, which could then be gotten with just an alias, instead of a real name.

Women seem to be more frequently targeted by trolls and bullies than men.

> **George Takei,** veteran *Star Trek* actor and equal rights advocate, offered to lend his surname as a substitute when a Tennessee Senate committee introduced a bill that would ban the use of the word "gay" in classrooms.

Anita Sarkeesian, host and creator of the Feminist Frequency YouTube videos, found herself a target of online vitriol when she began work on a series of videos examining sexist tropes in video games. She was accused of not being a real gamer, of being a poor researcher, and of outright lying about the games she featured—all, the accusations went, to further her agenda. And these were some of the nicer comments: she also received rape and death threats, many of them credible enough to be taken seriously by the FBI.

Online bullying is often dismissed as relatively harmless by people referencing the good old schoolyard aphorism "Sticks and stones may break my bones, but names will never hurt me." But the effects of online bullying are devastating. More than 22 million teens are bullied online each year, and thousands have committed suicide as a result of a combination of factors, online bullying being one of them. Cyberbullying has become an epidemic, and law enforcement now treats it as a serious breach.

But just as the internet provides cover for trolls and bullies and their obnoxious acts, it can also host and promote support groups. In response to the bullying (both online and in real life) that gay youth so often have to deal with, an organization was formed to encourage and empower kids and young adults by instilling them with the belief that life will actually get better and that there is no shame in being gay. The It Gets Better Project created a series of videos of famous gay people and allies speaking candidly about their own experiences to let young people know they are not alone.

Men's rights activists used the hashtag #notallmen to protest against the labeling of men as rapists or potential abusers. When Elliot Rodger went on a shooting rampage spurred by his misogynist sentiments, people (men, too, but mostly women) countered with

#yesallwomen—a conscious reversal of #notallmen—to point out the sexism women face every day, sexism that many men aren't even aware of.

Sexism affects women of all ages. When a little girl was told by a shoe-store employee that the Clarks dinosaur shoes she wanted were only for boys, female scientists posted pictures of their shoes while at work with the tag #inmyshoes.

Social media has made the Internet a cacophonous place, sometimes a frightening and toxic place, but it can also be supportive and surprisingly protective.

DATA IS FOREVER

HOW SECURE ARE YOU?

The idea that our data is only available to those we share it with sounds good, but is unfortunately not true. Even with the best encryption, there are always ways to steal data, as there are ways to convince people to give it away willingly. Nearly everything posted on the Internet remains indefinitely, even after you have deleted it.

Consider the good old email. Most email providers don't encrypt data, although many of them offer it as an added feature. In the early days of Internet, intercepting emails was the easiest way to steal data—and, since data can be replicated infinitely without affecting the original, the theft would go unnoticed. And that's only one of many ways to steal an email. Emails can be lifted from a provider's servers, or stolen from the sender's or receiver's computer. Even when emails are deleted, they tend to sit in a virtual trash bin for some time before they are actually purged.

Social media can be thought of in much the same way. Your profile is stored in your computer's memory for easy access. That same information can also be stored, however temporarily, in the memory of the computers of others who view it. And it is also stored on the servers of social media platforms, ready for transmittal.

All social media platforms have privacy settings and security features, but users often have to actively opt in to them. You can make your entire account private, available only to those you have designated as "friends," or decide to elect individual posts as either private or public. But if someone is determined to steal your information, there are ways to hack social media accounts, just as there are ways to hack emails.

Concerns about users' privacy—everything from personal information like someone's name and address, to less identifiable but valuable data like someone's shopping habits or news preferences—have led to increased security concerns. Facebook continuously tweaks and updates its privacy settings, but it also doesn't want to make Facebook profiles too private, because user preferences fuel advertising—which is how Facebook makes money.

For the average user, allowing some personal data to be accessed by apps and services can actually improve the social media experience. By knowing which feeds you follow, Twitter can tailor its suggestions of people and organizations you might want to follow, and serve you ads for products and services you're actually interested in.

For users who require anonymity, like activist groups, the less information collected, the better. For those users, social media that place weight on secrecy and security are more attractive, as are services that permit the creation of accounts under pseudonyms (something Facebook is gradually weeding out, but which Google+ added after originally requiring verifiable names to register).

SEXTING

When Snapchat debuted, one of its most attractive features was that shared images could be seen only by the sender and the receiver and, once viewed, self-delete. There are, of course, ways to hack that feature—like using another device to take a screenshot while the image is being viewed on the app. The proclaimed privacy of apps like Snapchat and Telegram makes them appealing to those who like to "sext" (send text messages with sexual

DID YOU KNOW

Trojan horse software is named for the wooden horse in the ancient Greek epic poem *The Odyssey* that the Greeks built and left as a gift for the Trojans, who then pulled the sculpture inside their city walls. At night, Greek soldiers crept out of the giant horse and opened the gates to their compatriots. Similarly, Trojan horse software infects a user's computer, disguised within a seemingly legitimate program, then opens a back door for a hacker to access the computer.

content and images) or send "dick pics" (photographs of male genitals, usually, but not always, the sender's own, often sent unsolicited to women).

Sexting and dick pics can easily go awry, as the whole world saw when the aptly named Anthony Weiner, then a US representative from New York City, sent pictures of himself partly naked at the gym to a female Twitter follower. The images went public and a scandal erupted, eventually forcing the congressman to resign. The incident illustrates how easily a simple mistake can ruin the life of a seemingly intelligent person (although it was later revealed that Weiner had sent similar photos to other women, both before and after this incident). Although Weiner recovered from his error enough to run for mayor of New York City in 2013, those images will almost certainly remain online for anyone to find, and he will always be remembered as the politician whose sexts went public.

OFFICIAL WATCHERS

Users concerned with protecting their privacy can elect to limit access to their accounts, disable third-party services' access, and turn off the location-tracking functions of their devices. Those measures may keep information private, but they will not completely disable the apps from collecting that data. And such measures will certainly not keep the government out.

The United States and other governments are interested in monitoring social media to collect data and conduct surveillance. Basic social media monitoring software can only yield as much data as the user makes available (although most users are unaware how much information is actually public and how even general information can be statistically processed to reveal more about the user). The information most people post online is seldom anything that couldn't also be found in real life. It just happens the digital data aggregation is easier than flipping through phone books and newspapers, talking to neighbors, and using other analog sources.

Governments have introduced legislation to enable them to spy directly on citizens. In 2007 it was revealed that the FBI had developed a Trojan horse software, called Magic Lantern, that could infect computers and record users' keystrokes, allowing the FBI to obtain passwords and gain access to users' accounts. The United Kingdom has adopted a policy that allows police to access people's computers remotely, without a warrant, if the authorities believe that such surveillance can be used to prevent criminal activity.

> *Governments have introduced legislation to enable them to spy directly on citizens.*

If users treated the Internet and social media as other public spaces, posting only information that they would gladly share in real life, the dangers of being online would be greatly diminished. The real issue is those spur-of-the-moment posts people make without thinking—the stupid things they do in anger, or because they seem funny at the time, or because everybody else is doing it. In real life, a careless comment, a racist remark, a rude gesture, or even a bully's abuse can soon fade away and be forgotten. The people directly involved may never forget it, but others around them will. Online, on the other hand, impulsive remarks can live forever. Even after they've been deleted, they might be recorded on someone else's computer for later use, or archived somewhere like in the Internet Archive's Wayback Machine. And, for people who are famous, with thousands and millions of followers, a stupid comment can haunt for a very long time. Even if the person deletes the comment, chances are people who responded didn't delete their responses. The more followers a person has, the likelier it is someone took a screenshot of the offensive, insensitive, or racist thing that was posted.

It lately has become fashionable for teens to sext each other. Apps—like Snapchat—that are supposed to be secure and automatically delete posts can make it seem like sexts are safe. But when someone uses a hack to save the comment or photo, or simply rephotographs it with another device, what was supposed to have been ephemeral becomes permanent. Sexts can also be passed around and the people engaged in the communication mocked and bullied. Solving this problem requires awareness: Let people know how technology works, explain the limitations of privacy and hope that they will then make more informed decisions.

DANGEROUS EMAIL

Less easy to deal with, and potentially more harmful, are the activities of hackers who break into computer networks to steal data. Part of a larger company that makes software and devices, Sony is familiar with being hacked. And yet, Sony's PlayStation network has been hacked multiple times, making the company aware of how good hackers can be. And recently, hackers got into Sony Pictures' network, perhaps with help from ex-employees, and downloaded a mind-boggling amount of data, including emails and digital files containing unreleased movies.

Once released to the public, those emails—many containing character-damaging (and career-damaging) private conversations—are published and scrutinized. The same holds true of movies downloaded for free; in fact, the spread of electronic files is impossible to thwart.

Sometimes emails don't even need to be released to cause trouble. In March 2015 it was revealed that, while Hillary Clinton was US Secretary of State, she used an unencrypted email system—one hosted on her own home server—instead of the official provided by the government. The concern was that, by using her own email, Clinton had engaged in business that she wanted to keep secret from the prying eyes of the State Department. Clinton immediately sent thousands of pages of emails (although not all) to the State Department, asking that they be made public to prove that she had nothing to hide and had engaged in nothing wrong. Will Clinton's choice to use her private account compromise her chances of getting elected? It remains to be seen.

A LITTLE BIRDIE TOLD ME

Use of social media has been continually increasing in the Middle East and northern Africa as people see how it can be a powerful force for social change.

MOROCCO

7.4
MILLION

(22% of population)

TUNISIA

4.6
MILLION

(42% of population)

ALGERIA

7
MILLION

(18% of population)

LIBYA

1.9
MILLION

(30% of population)

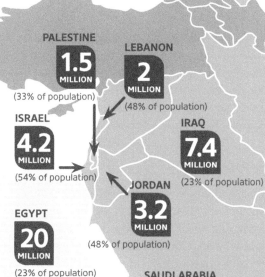

PALESTINE
1.5 MILLION
(33% of population)

LEBANON
2 MILLION
(48% of population)

ISRAEL
4.2 MILLION
(54% of population)

IRAQ
7.4 MILLION
(23% of population)

KUWAIT
1.5 MILLION
(49% of population)

JORDAN
3.2 MILLION
(48% of population)

EGYPT
20 MILLION
(23% of population)

QATAR
1.3 MILLION
(56% of population)

SAUDI ARABIA
8.6 MILLION
(31% of population)

UNITED ARAB EMIRATES
4.8 MILLION
(51% of population)

YEMEN
1.6 MILLION
(6% of population)

ANONYMOUS

HOW HACKTIVISTS WORK

F or the average user, the Internet is a place where complete anonymity is hard to attain. Many social media platforms and forums allow users to post under aliases, and a few offer anonymous posting. But most sites require at least an email address, and even anonymous posts leave a trace of the user's IP address. Hackers, however, are not average users.

BEING ANONYMOUS

For a hacker, it is possible to achieve almost complete anonymity online. Hackers come in a variety of types, but are commonly divided into "white hat" and "black hat"—those who hack for a good cause, and those who do it for malicious or purely selfish reasons. Hackers are categorized more by their intentions than by their actions.

WikiLeaks, for example, is a repository of information provided voluntarily by outside informants. The people running the website believe the public has the right to information to be collected; so they provide a platform for all that information and publish it for all to see. Governments are understandably uneasy about WikiLeaks and similar organizations.

Right: Julian Assange at the Occupy London demonstration was cautioned by police, October 15, 2011.

To guarantee the impartiality of the information and the protection of the whistle-blowers, Wikileaks uses a secure online "drop box," where users can deposit files. The site itself remains "uncensorable" as its servers are scattered all over the world. It is mainly hosted in Sweden where servers are given legal protection. It would be almost impossible for the authorities of any one country to shut down WikiLeaks.

Another precursor to social media is IRC, or Internet Relay Chat. IRC allows groups of like-minded individuals to gather in a virtual space and talk about their interests. IRC can be used relatively anonymously and is good for groups concerned with protecting their privacy because users have to ask to join an IRC channel. Although IRC itself has no mechanism for file sharing, the various clients (that is, software) for using IRC can implement file sharing—usually Direct Client-to-Client (DCC) transfers. The anonymity of IRC means it is often used to pass around pirated books, movies, and software.

ACTING ANONYMOUSLY

In its early days, the group called "Anonymous" was thought to be made up of immature pranksters doing things "for the lulz" (derived from the online shorthand "LOL" for "laughing out loud"). Its members posted on the /b/ section of 4chan, known for its shocking content, and users referred to themselves as /b/tards. This was the Anonymous that hacked the Epilepsy Foundation's website, changing its forum link to one for an image of flashing colored lights—an image that can trigger an epileptic episode.

But, over time, the campaigns organized by Anonymous have become less about the lulz and more about social justice. Some

members have pretended to be under-
age girls to entrap pedophiles. Others
hacked emails and social media to obtain
evidence against the young men accused
of the 2012 Steubenville, Ohio, rape case,
eventually sending evidence to police.

By then, the group had matured
beyond 4chan and began using IRC to
meet and organize. It used massive DDoS
attacks ("Dedicated Denial of Service"
attacks) that bombard a website with
a vast number of visits in a very short
period to overwhelm and shut down the
server. The group also used file-sharing
sites, like Megaupload, to distribute
encryption software and information
useful to dissidents in countries protesting repressive regimes.

Still, some Anonymous members
thought the group had become way too
politicized and wanted to return to its
irreverent roots. In 2011 several members
broke away and formed LulzSec (short for
Lulz Security), and began to attack people
and sites for the sheer fun of it. In May
and June 2011, LulzSec went on a hacking
spree, attacking everyone from Sony, to
the US Senate website, to an Arizona
law enforcement agency and even the
CIA. In mid-June, LulzSec disbanded and

MIRROR MIRROR

*The black mirror
in the title of the
TV series* Black
Mirror *refers to the
ubiquitous screens—
television, computer
monitor, tablet, and
smartphone—that
command our
attention every day.
When these devices
are powered off, they
form a blank, black
rectangle that in the
case of phones and
tablets is reflective,
like a mirror. These
devices have become
the means by which
we see ourselves and
one another—they
reflect our real lives
in a virtual life.*

re-formed back inside Anonymous as AntiSec, a less lulz-oriented, more political hacking group.

THE FACE OF ANONYMOUS

The Guy Fawkes mask used by Anonymous has its origins in 1605, when an antigovernment agitator named Guy Fawkes attempted, along with a group of co-conspirators, to blow up the English Houses of Parliament. Some of the conspirators had second thoughts, fearing innocent bystanders might get hurt, and one of them sent an anonymous letter to the authorities warning of the Gunpowder Plot, as it is known. On November 5, Guy Fawkes happened to be in the cellar of the House of Lords with the gunpowder when it was stormed by government forces. He was caught, tortured, and finally executed. Since then, England has celebrated Guy Fawkes Night, or Bonfire Night, every November 5.

Whatever the connotations of the actual Guy Fawkes persona, it was forever stamped on the popular imaginary by the movie *V for Vendetta*, based on the much-lauded graphic novel by Alan Moore and David Lloyd. In the movie, a man known only as "V" fights against a repressive, Orwellian, dystopian near-future government. Like Guy Fawkes, he decides to blow up the Parliament, which has become a symbol of repression and tyranny. Just before the crucial date (November 5, of course), he distributes Guy Fawkes masks and capes to millions of citizens, and asks them to show up and witness the downfall of the government.

[
Documentaries about social media include *#140 Characters, InRealLife, Generation Social, Startup.com, Terms and Conditions May Apply,* and *We Live in Public.*
]

Initially, the Guy Fawkes mask was adopted by Anonymous on the online imageboard 4chan, where a popular stick-figure cartoon character Epic Fail Guy started showing up in posts wearing the mask. It became a popular symbol for dissidents, when Anonymous orchestrated an anti-Scientology protest.

As the politics of Anonymous evolved, so too did the connotation of the mask, until it finally became the identifying symbol of anti-authoritarianism. Mask wearers have shown up at protests against autocratic regimes around the world.

CHEAP
CHEEP
SHOTS

#WhyIStayed When football star Ray Rice was caught on camera hitting his then-fiancée, one woman started the #WhyIStayed hashtag to encourage awareness about spousal abuse. Unfortunately, the person responsible for DiGiorno Pizza's social media didn't bother to find out what the tag was about before tweeting "#WhyIStayed You had pizza." The backlash was instantaneous and DiGiorno had to quickly delete the tweet and apologize. To its credit, DiGiorno spent a lot of time responding to those who were offended.

#MyNYPD The New York City Police Department tried to use Twitter to improve its image by asking users to tweet photographs of themselves with NYPD officers using the tag #MyNYPD. This hashtag was meant to inspire happy posts showing how nice police officers are. Instead, Twitter users took over the tag to show images of police brutality.

THROUGH A GLASS, DARKLY

OUR SCREENS, OURSELVES

t is telling that the movie from which the hacktivist group
Anonymous took its most recognizable public symbol actually
doesn't feature social media at all. Instead, in *V for Vendetta*,
the antiauthoritarian messages from the government are spread
by much older technology: television and snail mail. But social
media not only affects our real-world lives, it transform our
entertainment culture too. Social media has become so ubiquitous that it would seem an oversight for TV shows and movies
to ignore its existence instead of using Twitter, Facebook, or
YouTube as plot points.

Recent movies revolve around the rise of social media and the
lives of its founders. *The Social Network* dramatized the life of Mark
Zuckerberg from a hotheaded Harvard student, to programmer,
developer and businessman. Even without the sensationalism
of the movie, Zuckerberg and Facebook make a pretty dramatic
story: a small college social network developed by a misfit spreads
like wildfire and makes its founder both enormously rich and
equally loathed.

Less obvious uses of real-world social media events appear in TV series like *Law & Order* and its spin-offs (*Law & Order: Special Victims Unit* and *Law & Order: Criminal Intent*), which are known for being inspired by current headlines. Episodes have featured narrative stories about cyberbullying, sexting, the spread of child pornography through online forums, and the use of social media in tricking and trapping pedophiles. *Law & Order* has a tendency of casting social media in a negative light, as does the British series *Black Mirror,* which takes social media a step further into the speculative realm with *Twilight Zone*-like stories about a near-future society where people are influenced by social media in ways detrimental to their humanity.

Movies have also made various uses of social media. At least two films—*Birdman* and *Chef*—look at how a refusal to engage on social media can affect people's prospects. Each day, artists, writers, and other creatives feel pressured to be active on social media to remind the world that they exist. In these two movies, the main characters' social media abstinence costs them their personal and professional success. Gone are the days, it seems, of reclusive artists living outside of the social sphere but venerated for their genius.

Social media's influence is also felt in news, where Twitter posts add a personal dimension to news stories and channels encourage viewers to continue their discussions about current affairs in their various social networks. Then there's reality TV. For some time, reality TV shows—in particular those with a voting feature—have pleaded for viewers' input. In the beginning, viewers had to call on the phone to register their vote; later, they could vote on websites. Finally, a lot of that engagement moved to social media, via text messages and Twitter mentions, YouTube shares, and Facebook likes.

FREEDOM! FOREVER!
NATALIE PORTMAN HUGO WEAVING
V FOR VENDETTA
AN UNCOMPROMISING VISION OF THE FUTURE
FROM THE CREATORS OF THE MATRIX TRILOGY

THE SUPREME COURT OF PUBLIC OPINION

GETTING IT RIGHT

For all the terrible things one hears about social media—the bullying, trolling, hacking, and videos of violence—it's impossible to deny that the apps and websites we use every day are responsible for a lot of

Right: Grumpy Cat looking unimpressed with Senator Cory Booker (D-N.J.)

good in the world. The use of Twitter and Facebook to organize protests against repressive regimes and demand better conditions for workers has ushered in a new wave of activism. Individual users can work together to create a common voice. And, even those with huge social media followings start small.

Before the 2008 presidential election, no national electoral campaign had been run using social media. Previous candidates had made use of technologies available to them—newspapers, radio, and television. But in 2008, MySpace was still popular and Facebook was on the rise, and then-Senator Barack Obama had the idea of using social media—Facebook, especially—to connect with voters and build support for his campaign of hope and change. In addition to trying to organize people, Obama and his team let people organize themselves. The freedom and self-governance of social media fit well with Obama's message, and Facebook helped him win the election.

If voters can rally behind a relatively unknown politician because he can make them believe in a better future via Facebook, how much more effective can a popular actor from a beloved science

FOR WHO?

While the name "Anonymous" seems obvious, its origin is a little more complicated. The group originated on the imageboard 4chan (an imageboard is an online bulletin board focused mainly on images), where users who did not choose a nickname were given the default screen name "Anonymous."

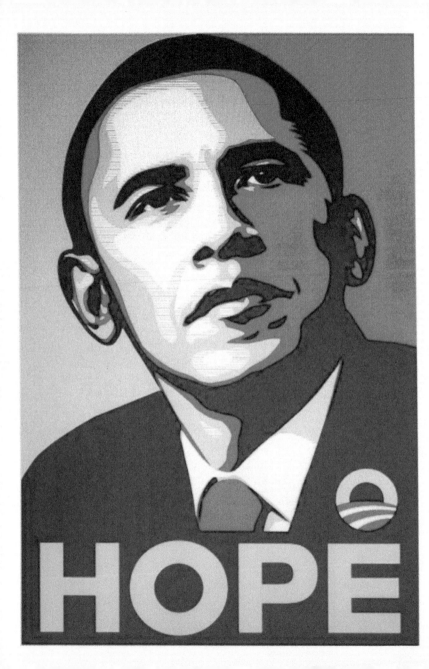

fiction television series be? *Star Trek's* George Takei had been on Twitter for some time, but joined Facebook in 2011, seeking a better way to connect with fans. He has posted a mix of funny memes and links to articles about human rights in general, and gay rights in particular. His millions of fans seem to like the mix.

Social media has also become a good place, counterintuitively, for intelligent commentary on the world. It is a great place for lay audiences to find out about unfamiliar topics, like specific sciences. Social media whizzes have employed Facebook, Twitter, Tumblr, YouTube, and other platforms to show how cool and accessible science can be.

Neil deGrasse Tyson, an astrophysicist and director of the Hayden Planetarium in New York City, tirelessly campaigns for science education. His enthusiasm for science of all disciplines, especially astrophysics, is infectious. He posts regularly on Facebook, often using current events—from the Super Bowl to the "supermoon"—to connect science with the everyday, and make it even more than it already is.

Another spacey science fan, and Canadian national hero, is astronaut Chris Hadfield, veteran of shuttle missions and the first Canadian commander of the International Space Station. While on the ISS, he began posting photographs shot in space

Who's winning the Internet? That colloquialism gets thrown around plenty, but there are actually winners, at least according to the annual Webby Awards, which honor "the best of the Internet." The awards recognize the best websites, movies, mobile sites and apps, advertising and media, online film and video, and special achievements. The 2015 winners included *Last Week Tonight* and the #LikeAGirl campaign, which encouraged women to post photos highlighting their talents (a riff on the taunt, "you throw like a girl").

US President Barack Obama poses for a selfie with Bill Nye, left, and Neil DeGrasse Tyson. February 28, 2014 in Washington, DC.

to his Tumblr and Twitter accounts. He quickly gained a large following all over the world; he showed people their world from a perspective few have ever gotten the chance to see. Hadfield also shot videos of seemingly ordinary things that space makes extraordinary: wringing water from a washcloth in the ISS's zero gravity, or showing what happens when you cry in space. His YouTube channel, much like his Tumblr before, quickly grew in popularity.

Museums gained a voice when a student at the University of Montana started a YouTube series called *The Brain Scoop*. Emily Graslie showed what happened behind the scenes at a small zoological museum—everything from de-fleshing roadkill skeletons to make a new specimen, to a basement full of jars containing preserved fish. Graslie's mission was to celebrate museums; she also became a role model for young women in science, technology, engineering, and math (STEM) fields. Graslie's little show about a little museum gained so many followers that Chicago's famed Field Museum of Natural History offered her a job—even gave her the title "Chief Curiosity Correspondent"—allowing her to continue to spread her love for science and education to a wider audience.

Of course, not everyone resorts to social media to change the world. Some change the way things are done simply in their field. When Beyoncé was ready to release a new album in 2013, instead of going through the usual hype of advance advertising, she kept the whole process secret. When everything was ready, she simply posted her album cover on Instagram with the message "Surprise!" Her plan was to go straight to her fans and let them do the hyping. And they did. The album sold 430,000 digital copies on iTunes in the first 24 hours.

However one might feel about Facebook or Twitter, YouTube or Tumblr, social media is here to stay—at least until the next big technological revolution. We can ignore it or embrace it, but simply cannot deny its life-changing and world-changing power.

DID YOU KNOW

One of the "actorvist" crowd, Amy Poehler has built an immense online community with Amy Poehler's Smart Girls. The group boasts more than 1.5 million members from countries around the world, and bills itself as a place where girls can be themselves on the internet, without feeling the societal pressures of major fashion sites or be subjected to bullying from their peers. The Smart Girls' motto is, "Change the world by being yourself."

A PARTING
THOUGHT

"We are anonymous. We represent freedom. We oppose oppression. We are simply an evolution of the technological system. Where liberty is at risk, expect us."

—ANONYMOUS, HACKTIVIST COLLECTIVE

BIBLIOGRAPHY

Adbusters. "#OCCUPYWALLSTREET." July 13, 2011. Accessed April 3, 2015. www.adbusters.org/blogs/adbusters-blog/occupywallstreet.html.

Agiesta, Jennifer. "Poll: Hillary Clinton's Email Divides Public." CNN. March 16, 2015. Accessed April 5, 2015. www.cnn.com/2015/03/16/politics /hillary-clinton-email-poll-2016/.

Alexa. "The Top 500 Sites on the Web." Accessed March 30, 2015. www. alexa.com/topsites.

American Civil Liberties Union. "Reform the Patriot Act." Accessed March 29, 2015. www.aclu.org/reform-patriot-act

Anderson, Kurt. "Person of the Year 2011: The Protestor." Time. December 14, 2011. Accessed April 3, 2015. content.time.com/time/specials /packages/article/0,28804,2101745_2102132,00.html.

Anderson, Lisa. "Demystifying the Arab Spring: Parsing the Differences Between Tunisia, Egypt, and Libya." Foreign Affairs. May/June 2011. Accessed March 31, 2015. www.foreignaffairs.com/articles/67693 /lisa-anderson/demystifying-the-arab-spring.

Andras, S.H. "Study: Facebook Dominates in Middle East." Social Times. April 25, 2014. Accessed April 6, 2015. www.adweek.com/socialtimes /study-facebook-dominates-in-middle-east/298999

API Voice. "Twitter Acquisitions." July 9, 2012. Accessed April 6, 2015. apivoice.com/2012/07/09/twitter-acquisitions/.

AppCrawlr. "100+ Top Apps for Social Photo (iPhone/iPad)." Accessed March 28, 2015. appcrawlr.com/ios-apps/best-apps-social-photo

Avalaunch Media. "The Complete History of Social Media." Accessed March 24, 2015. avalaunchmedia.com/history-of-social-media/Main.html

Bajjada, Cheyenne Lourdes. "Is Social Media Not Only Changing Our Lives but Also the Movies and TV Shows We Watch?" Movie Pilot. March 13, 2015. Accessed April 6, 2015. moviepilot.com/posts/2015/03/13/is -social-media-not-only-changing-our-lives-but-also-the-movies -and-tv-we-watch-2776478.

Barbaro, Michael. "Brooklyn Congressman Won't Quit Mayor's Race." The New York Times. October 14, 2008. Accessed April 5, 2015. www.nytimes.com/2008/10/15/nyregion/15weiner.html.

Barna, Maxwell. "The FBI Is Hiding Details About an Alleged Occupy Houston Assassination Plot." Vice News. March 21, 2014. Accessed April 3, 2015. news.vice.com/article/the-fbi-is-hiding-details-about -an-alleged-occupy-houston-assassination-plot.

Barrett, Devlin. "Democrats Push Weiner to Go." The Wall Street Journal. June 9, 2011. Accessed April 5, 2015. www.wsj.com/articles /SB10001424052702304392704576374014222200024.

Basu, Saikat. "What Are Browser Cache and Cookies, and Does Clearing Them Help?" Guiding Tech. Accessed April 5, 2015. www.guidingtech. com/8925/what-are-browser-cache-cookies-does-clearing-them-help/.

BBC. "The Interview: A Guide to the Cyber Attack on Hollywood." BBC News. December 29, 2014. Accessed April 3, 2015. www.bbc.com /news/entertainment-arts-30512032.

———. BBC. "Instagram Blocks Some Drugs Advert Tags After BBC Probe." BBC News. November 7, 2013. Accessed April 3, 2015. www.bbc.com /news/technology-24842750.

———."NYPD Twitter Campaign 'Backfires' After Hashtag Hijacked." BBC News, April 23, 2014. Accessed April 3, 2015. www.bbc.com/news /technology-27126041.

———. "Turkey Clashes: Why Are Gezi Park and Taksim Square So Important?" BBC News. June 7, 2013. Accessed March 31, 2015.

———. "Thailand PM 'to Replace Martial Law' with New Restrictions." BBC News. March 31, 2015. Accessed March 31, 2015. www.bbc.com /news/world-asia-32126761.

———. "Why Is Thailand Under Military Rule?" BBC News, May 22, 2014. Accessed March 31, 2015. www.bbc.com/news/world-asia-25149484.

———. "Arab Uprising: Country by Country - Tunisia." BBC News. December 16, 2013. Accessed March 31, 2015. www.bbc.com/news /world-12482315 .

———. "Syria: The Story of the Conflict." BBC News. March 12, 2015. Accessed March 31, 2015. www.bbc.com/news/world-middle -east-26116868.

Beauchamp, Zack. "Myth #3: ISIS Is Part of al-Qaeda." The 9 Biggest Myths about ISIS. Vox. October 1, 2015. Accessed March 31, 2015. www.vox. com/cards/isis-myths-iraq/al-qaeda-isis.

Bennett, Shea. "The History of Social Networking Through the Ages." June 26, 2014. Accessed March 24, 2015. www.adweek.com /socialtimes/social-networking-ages/499633

———. "The Ten Biggest Social Networks Worldwide." Social¬Times. December 24, 2014. Accessed March 30, 2015. www.adweek.com /socialtimes/largest-social-networks-worldwide/504044.

Bershadker, Matthew. "Let's #OpentheBarns to Transparency." Huffington Post. March 27, 2015. Accessed March 29, 2015. www.huffingtonpost.com/matt-bershadker/lets-openthebarns-to-tran_b_6958138.html

Betters, Elyse. "What Does Facebook Own? Here's the Companies It Has Acquired and the Reasons Why." Pocket-lint. April 26, 2014. Accessed April 6, 2015. www.pocket-lint.com/news/128617-what-does-facebook-own-here-s-the-companies-it-has-acquired-and-the-reasons-why.

Blanchard, Madison. " 'It Just Went Wild:' #FoundBunny at Halifax Museum Creates Twitter Buzz." Metro News Halifax. March 23, 2015. Accessed March 24, 2015. metronews.ca/news/halifax/1320827/foundbunny-at-halifax-museum-creates-twitter-buzz/.

Blodget, Henry. "Charts: Here's What the Wall Street Protesters Are So Angry About…" Business Insider. October 11, 2011. Accessed April 3, 2015. www.businessinsider.com/what-wall-street-protesters-are-so-angry-about-2011-10.

Bobic, Igor. "Hillary Clinton Responds to Email Controversy: 'I Want the Public to See My Email.'" The Huffington Post. March 5, 2015. Accessed April 5, 2015. www.huffingtonpost.com/2015/03/05/hillary-clinton-email-state_n_6805478.html.

Bonfirenight.net. "Guy Fawkes and Bonfire Night." Accessed April 5, 2015. www.bonfirenight.net/iimdex.php.

BuzzFeed. "About BuzzFeed." Accessed April 1, 2014. www.buzzfeed.com/about.

Canadian Civil Liberties Association. "(Un)Lawful Access: Stop Online Spying." Accessed March 29, 2015. ccla.org/our-work/public-safety/privacy/unlawful-access-top-online-spying/

Canadian Press, The. "Link Between Cyberbullying and Teen Suicides Oversimplified, Experts Say." Maclean's. December 15, 2013. Accessed April 3, 2015. www.macleans.ca/news/canada/link-between-cyberbullying-and-teen-suicides-oversimplified-experts-say/.

Carlson, Nicholas. "The Real History of Twitter." Business Insider. April 13, 2011. Accessed March 28, 2015. www.businessinsider.com/how-twitter-was-founded-2011-4

Carr, David. "How Obama Tapped into Social Networks' Power." The New York Times. November 9, 2008. Accessed April 6, 2015. www.nytimes.com/2008/11/10/business/media/10carr.html.

Casey, Ralph D. "What is Propaganda?" July 1944. American Historical Association. Accessed March 26, 2015. www.historians.org/about -aha-and-membership/aha-history-and-archives/gi-roundtable -series/pamphlets/what-is-propaganda.

Changing Works. "Propaganda." ChangingMinds.org. Accessed March 26, 2015. changingminds.org/techniques/propaganda/propaganda.htm

Chris Hadfield on YouTube. www.youtube.com/user/ColChrisHadfield.

Churchill, Ward and Jim Vander Wall. The COINTELPRO Papers: Documents from the FBI's Secret Wars Against Dissent in the United States. South End Press. Accessed March 30, 2015. archive.is/YJA4m.

Collins, Ian. "5 Common Uses for Social Networking and the Effect on Your Target Audience." Blogussion. Accessed March 24, 2015. www.blogussion.com/general/uses-social-networking/.

Constine, Josh. "Ello Pretends It's Not Over with Video and Music Launch." TechCrunch. January 22, 2015. Accessed March 28, 2015. techcrunch. com/2015/01/22/remember-ello-no-i-dont-either/.

Costill, Albert. "The Top 25 Movies About Social Media." Search Engine Journal. February 20, 2014. Accessed April 6, 2015. www. searchenginejournal.com/top-25-movies-social-media/90253/.

Cox, Savannah. "25 of Neil DeGrasse Tyson's Most Mind Blowing Tweets." All That Is Interesting. May 18, 2014. Accessed April 6, 2015. all-that-is-interesting.com/neil-degrasse-tyson-tweets#1

Crystal, Garry. "Police Computer Hacking Powers and Civil Liberties." Civil Rights Movement UK. March 27, 2015. Accessed April 5, 2015. www.civilrightsmovement.co.uk/police-computer-hacking -powers-civil-liberties.html.

DeviantArt. "Premium Member Benefits." Accessed March 28, 2015. www.deviantart.com/checkout/?mx=premium&subpref=22870_0.

Digital Trends. "The History of Social Networking." August 5, 2014. Accessed March 24, 2015. www.digitaltrends.com/features /the-history-of-social-networking/

Dredge, Stuart. "The Top 50 Apps for Creative Minds." The Guardian. March 22, 2015. Accessed March 28, 2015. www.theguardian.com /technology/2015/mar/22/the-top-50-apps-for-creative-minds
———.YouTube Aims to Tame the Trolls with Changes to its Comments Section." The Guardian. November 7, 2013. Accessed April 3, 2015. www.theguardian.com/technology/2013/nov/07/you¬tube-comments -trolls-moderation-google.

Drenovsky, Rachael, et al. "American Abolitionism." 2002-2008. Accessed March 27, 2015. americanabolitionist.liberalarts.iupui.edu/

Dutta, Soumitra, and Matthew Fraser. "Barack Obama and the Facebook Election." US News & World Report. November 19, 2008. Accessed April 6, 2015. www.usnews.com/opinion/articles/2008/11/19 /barack-obama-and-the-facebook-election.

Dyer, Evan. "How ISIS Is Different from al-Qaeda." CBC News. March 29, 2015. Accessed March 31, 2015. www.cbc.ca/news/politics /how-isis-is-different-from-al-qaeda-1.3001969.

eBizMBA. "Top 15 Most Popular Social Networking Sites: March 2015." Accessed March 30, 2015. www.ebizmba.com/articles/social -networking-websites.

Editors of Encyclopaedia Britannica. "Arab Spring." Encyclopaedia Britannica. Last updated January 13, 2015. Accessed March 31, 2015. www.britannica.com/EBchecked/topic/1784922/Arab-Spring.

Editors of Matter. "About Matter." Accessed April 1, 2015. medium.com /matter/about.

Eyewitness to History. "Loose Lips Sink Ships." 1997. Accessed March 29, 2015. www.eyewitnesstohistory.com

Federal Bureau of Investigation. "Definitions of Terrorism in the US Code." Accessed March 30, 2015. www.fbi.gov/about-us/investigate /terrorism/terrorism-definition.

———. "Operation Backfire: Help Find Four Eco-Terrorists." November 19, 2008. Accessed March 30, 2015. www.fbi.gov/news/stories/2008 /november/backfire_11908.

Facebook. "Data Policy." Last updated January 30, 2015. Accessed April 5, 2015. www.facebook.com/policy.php.

———. "How Do I Use Hashtags?" Facebook Help Center. Accessed April 3, 2015. www.facebook.com/help/587836257914341.

Fairchild, Caroline, and Jillian Berman. "How 7 Occupy Wall Street Issues Stack Up 2 Years Later." Huffington Post Business. September 18, 2013. Accessed April 3, 2015. www.huffingtonpost.com/2013/09/17 /occupy-wall-street-issues_n_3937483.html.

Flood, Alison. "Sock Puppetry and Fake Reviews: Publish and Be Damned." The Guardian. September 4, 2012. Accessed March 28, 2015. www.theguardian.com/books/2012/sep/04/sock-puppetry-publish -be-damned.

Gautney, Heather. "What is Occupy Wall Street? The History of Leaderless Movements." The Washington Post. October 10, 2011. Accessed May 18, 2015. www.washingtonpost.com/national/on-leadership/what-is -occupy-wall-street-the-history-of-leaderless-movements/2011 /10/10/gIQAwkFjaL_story.html.

Gazin-Schwartz, Amy. "What the Islamic State's Destruction of Antiq- uities Means to Archaeologists." New Republic. March 18, 2015. Accessed March 31, 2015. www.newrepublic.com/article/121324 /isis-destroys-precious-historical-artifacts-all-not-lost.

Gewertz, Ken. "Albert Einstein, Civil Rights Activist." Harvard University Gazette. April 12, 2007. Accessed March 30, 2015. web.archive.org /web/20070529080415/http://www.news.harvard.edu/ gazette/2007/04.12/01-einstein.html.

Glanz, James, and John Markoff. "US Underwrites Internet Detour Around Censors." The New York Times. June 12, 2011. Accessed April 1, 2015. www.nytimes.com/2011/06/12/world/12internet.html.

GlobalDemocracy.org. "People Power: A Short Discussion on Group Dynamics." June 21, 2103. Accessed March 28, 2015. www. globaldemocracy.org/people-power-a-short-discussion- on-group-dynamics/.

Golbeck, Jennifer. "Internet Trolls Are Narcissists, Psychopaths, and Sadists." Psychology Today. September 18, 2014. Accessed April 3, 2015. www.psychologytoday.com/blog/your-online-secrets/201409 /internet-trolls-are-narcissists-psychopaths-and-sadists.

Griner, David. "DiGiorno Is Really, Really Sorry About Its Tweet Acciden- tally Making Light of Domestic Violence." AdWeek. September 9, 2014. Accessed April 3, 2015. www.adweek.com/adfreak/digiorno-really -really-sorry-about-its-tweet-accidentally-making-light-domestic -violence-159998.

Harling, Jordan. "Five Ways Social Media Has Been Used for Good." Reason Digital. August 15, 2013. Accessed March 24, 2015. reasondigital.com/advice-and-training/five-ways-social-media -has-been-used-for-good/.

Hashtags.org Website. Accessed April 3, 2015. www.hashtags.org.

Hathaway, Jay. "What Is Gamergate, and Why? An Explainer for Non- Geeks." Gawker. October 10, 2014. Accessed April 3, 2015. gawker.com /what-is-gamergate-and-why-an-explainer-for-non-geeks-1642909080.

Hendricks, Drew. "Complete History of Social Media: Then and Now." Small Business Trends. May 8, 2013. Accessed March 24, 2015. smallbiztrends.com/2013/05/the-complete-history-of-social-media-infographic.html

Hennessey, Kathleen. "Rep. Anthony Weiner Makes Resignation Official." Los Angeles Times. June 20, 2011. Accessed April 5, 2015. articles.latimes.com/2011/jun/20/news/la-pn-weiner-resignation-20110620.

Hill, Kashmir. "#McDStories: When a Hashtag Becomes a Bashtag." Forbes. January 24, 2012. Accessed April 3, 2015. www.forbes.com/sites/kashmirhill/2012/01/24/mcdstories-when-a-hashtag-becomes-a-bashtag/.

History.com. "Russian Revolution." Accessed March 27, 2015. www.history.com/topics/russian-revolution

Honigman, Brian. "How Location-Based Social Networks Are Changing the Game for Businesses." Entrepreneur. January 9, 2013. Accessed March 24, 2015.

Horsley, Scott. "The Income Gap: Unfair, or Are We Just Jealous?" NPR. January 14, 2012. Accessed April 3, 2015. web.archive.org/web/20140502234240/http://www.npr.org/2012/01/14/145213421/the-income-gap-unfair-or-are-we-just-jealous.

How-To Geek. "Hacker Hat Colors Explained: Black Hats, White Hats, and Gray Hats." Accessed April 5, 2015. www.howtogeek.com/157460/hacker-hat-colors-explained-black-hats-white-hats-and-gray-hats/.

Human Rights Campaign. "It's OK to Be Takei." HRC Blog. May 24, 2011. Accessed April 3, 2015. www.hrc.org/blog/entry/its-ok-to-be-takei.

Hunt, Lynn. "Prints and Propaganda in the French Revolution." History Today. Accessed March 27, 2015. www.historytoday.com/lynn-hunt/engraving-republic-prints-and-propaganda-french-revolution

IMDb. "Black Mirror (2011-)." Internet Movie Database. Accessed April 6, 2015. www.imdb.com/title/tt2085059/.

———. "Birdman: Or (The Unexpected Virtue of Ignorance) (2014)." Internet Movie Database. Accessed April 6, 2015. www.imdb.com/title/tt2562232/.

———. "Chef (2014)." Internet Movie Database. Accessed April 6, 2015. www.imdb.com/title/tt2883512/.

———. "Hard Candy (2005)." Internet Movie Database. Accessed April 6, 2015. www.imdb.com/title/tt0424136/.

———. "Law & Order (1990-2010)." Internet Movie Database. Accessed April 6, 2015. www.imdb.com/title/tt0098844/.

———. "Law & Order: Criminal Intent (2001-2011)." Internet Movie Database. Accessed April 6, 2015. www.imdb.com/title/tt0275140/.

———. "Law & Order: Special Victims Unit (1999-)." Internet Movie Database. Accessed April 6, 2015. www.imdb.com/title/tt0203259/.

IMDb. "Silicon Valley (2014-)." Internet Movie Database. Accessed April 6, 2015. www.imdb.com/title/tt2575988/.

———. "Rosewater (2014)." Internet Movie Database. Accessed April 6, 2015. www.imdb.com/title/tt2752688/.

———. "The Social Network (2010)." Internet Movie Database. Accessed April 6, 2015. www.imdb.com/title/tt1285016/.

———. "Unfriended (2014)." Internet Movie Database. Accessed April 6, 2015. www.imdb.com/title/tt3713166/.

———. "V for Vendetta (2005)." Internet Movie Database. Accessed April 6, 2015. www.imdb.com/title/tt0434409/.

Independent Media Center. "Secret Grand Jury Investigations Have Led to Indictments of 12." January 24, 2006. Accessed March 30, 2015. www.indymedia.org/en/2006/01/831928.shtml.

Indvik, Lauren. "Facebook and Twitter Advertising Tips for Your Business." Mashable. October 9, 2013. Accessed March 28, 2015. mashable.com/2013/10/09/facebook-twitter-advertising/.

Internet Archive. "FAQs." Accessed April 4, 2015. archive.org/about/faqs.php.

InternetSlang.com. "IRL." Accessed April 5, 2015. www.internetslang.com/IRL-meaning-definition.asp.

It Gets Better Project. "What Is the It Gets Better Project?" Accessed April 3, 2015. www.itgetsbetter.org/pages/about-it-gets-better-project/.

Kemp, Simon. "Social, Digital & Mobile in the Middle East." We Are Social. July 24, 2014. Accessed April 6, 2015. wearesocial.net/blog/2014/07/social-digital-mobile-middle-east/

Kiisel, Ty. "Is Social Media Shortening Our Attention Span?" Forbes. January 1, 2013. Accessed April 1, 2015. www.forbes.com/sites/tykiisel/2012/01/25/is-social-media-shortening-our-attention-span/.

Kim, Erin. "Twitter Unveils 'Cashtags' to Track Stock Symbols." CNN Money. July 31, 2012. Accessed April 3, 2015. money.cnn.com/2012/07/31/technology/twitter-cashtag/.

Kincaid, Jason. "Ning's Bubble Bursts: No More Free Networks, Cuts 40% of Staff." TechCrunch. April 15, 2010. Accessed March 28, 21015. techcrunch.com/2010/04/15/nings-bubble-bursts-no-more-free-networks-cuts-40-of-staff/.

Klosowski, Thorin. "How Facebook Uses Your Data to Target Ads, Even Offline." Lifehacker. April 11, 2013. Accessed April 5, 2015. lifehacker.com/5994380/how-facebook-uses-your-data-to-target-ads-even-offline.

Knapp, Alex. "How George Takei Conquered Facebook." Forbes. March 23, 2012. Accessed April 6, 2015. http://www.forbes.com/sites/alexknapp/2012/03/23/how-george-takei-conquered-facebook/.

Kricfalusi, Elizabeth. "The Twitter Hashtag: What Is It and How Do You Use It?" Tech for Luddites. Last updated January 23, 2015. Accessed March 24, 2015. techforluddites.com/the-twitter-hashtag-what-is-it-and-how-do-you-use-it/.

Kushner, David. The Masked Avengers: How Anonymous Incited Online Vigilantism from Tunisia to Ferguson." The New Yorker. September 8, 2014. Accessed April 5, 2015. www.newyorker.com/magazine/2014/09/08/masked-avengers.

Letsch, Constanze. "A Year After the Protests, Gezi Park Nurtures the Seeds of a New Turkey." The Guardian. May 29, 2014. Accessed March 31, 2015. www.theguardian.com/world/2014/may/29/gezi-park-year-after-protests-seeds-new-turkey.

Lewis, Kent. "How Social Media Networks Facilitate Identity Theft and Fraud." Entrepreneurs' Organization. Accessed March 24, 2015. www.eonetwork.org/octane-magazine/special-features/social-media-networks-facilitate-identity-theft-fraud.

"Liberty, Equality, Fraternity: Exploring the French Revolution." Roy Rosenzweig Center for History and New Media, and the American Social History Project. Accessed March 27, 2015. chnm.gmu.edu/revolution/

Lin, Doris. "What Are Ag-Gag Laws and Why Are They Dangerous?" About Animal Rights. Accessed March 29, 2015. animalrights.about.com/od/animallaw/a/What-Are-Ag-Gag-Laws-And-Why-Are-They-Dangerous.htm

Lindsey, Richard A. "What the Arab Spring Tells Us About the Future of Social Media in Revolutionary Movements." Small Wars Journal. July 29, 2013. Accessed March 31, 2015. smallwarsjournal.com/jrnl/art

/what-the-arab-spring-tells-us-about-the-future-of-social-media-in
-revolutionary-movements.

Lohmann, Raychelle Cassada. "Sexting Teens: A Picture with Conse-
quences." Psychology Today. March 30, 2011. Accessed April 5, 2015.
www.psychologytoday.com/blog/teen-angst/201103/sexting-teens.

Lohr, Steve. "How Privacy Vanishes Online." The New York Times. March
16, 2010. Accessed April 5, 2015. www.nytimes.com/2010/03/17
/technology/17privacy.html.

Lunden, Ingrid. "Durov, Out for Good from VK.com, Plans a Mobile Social
Network Outside Russia." TechCrunch. April 22, 2014. Accessed March
28, 2015. techcrunch.com/2014/04/22/durov-out-for-good-from-vk
-com-plans-a-mobile-social-network-outside-russia/

Luppicini, R. The Emerging Field of Technoself Studies. Hershey, Pa.: Information Science Reference, 2013.

Magid, Larry. "What Is Snapchat and Why Do Kids Love It and Parents
Fear It?" Forbes. May 1, 2013. Accessed April 5, 2015. www.forbes.com
/sites/larrymagid/2013/05/01/what-is-snapchat-and-why-do-kids
-love-it-and-parents-fear-it/.

Malik, Shiv, Sandra Laville, Elena Cresci, and Aisha Gani. "ISIS in Duel
with Twitter and YouTube to Spread Extremist Propaganda." The
Guardian. September 24, 2014. Accessed April 2, 2013. www.
theguardian.com/world/2014/sep/24/isis-twitter-youtube-message
-social-media-jihadi.

Manfreda, Primoz. "Arab Spring Uprisings: Country Guide to Arab
Uprisings." About Middle East Issues. Accessed March 31, 2015.
middleeast.about.com/od/humanrightsdemocracy/tp/Arab
-Spring-Uprisings.htm.

———. "Current Situation in the Middle East." About Middle East
Issues. Accessed March 31, 2015. middleeast.about.com/od
/humanrightsdemocracy/tp/Current-Situation-In-The-Middle
-East.htm.

———. "Definition of the Arab Spring." About Middle East Issues. Accessed
March 31, 2015. middleeast.about.com/od/humanrightsdemocracy
/a/Definition-Of-The-Arab-Spring.htm .

Manning, Sturt. "Why ISIS Destroys Antiquities." CNN. March 9, 2015.
Accessed March 31, 2015. www.cnn.com/2015/03/06/opinions
/manning-isis-antiquities/.

Markoff, John. "Searching for Silicon Valley." The New York Times. April 16. 2009. Accessed April 6, 2015. www.nytimes.com/2009/04/17/travel /escapes/17Amer.html.

Marrs, Megan. "Buying Twitter Followers: The (Cheap) Price of Friendship." The Wordstream Blog. May 16, 2013. Accessed March 28, 2015. www.wordstream.com/blog/ws/2013/05/16/buying-twitter-followers -cheap-price-friendship

Mashable. "Viral Video." Accessed April 5, 2015. mashable.com/category /viral-video/.

O'Neill, Megan. "What Makes a Video 'Viral'?" Social Times. May 9, 2011. Accessed April 5, 2015. www.adweek.com/socialtimes/what-makes -a-video-viral/62414.

Medina, Jennifer. "Campus Killings Set Off Anguished Conversation About the Treatment of Women." The New York Times. May 26, 2014. Accessed April 3, 2015. www.nytimes.com/2014/05/27/us/campus-killings-set -off-anguished-conversation-about-the-treatment-of-women.html.

Merriam-Webster. "Counterintelligence." Accessed March 30, 2015. www.merriam-webster.com/dictionary/counterintelligence.

———. "Social Media." Accessed March 24, 2015. www.merriam-webster. com/dictionary/social%20media

Messina, Chris (@chrismessina). Twitter post. August 23, 2007. Accessed April 3, 2015. twitter.com/chrismessina/status/223115412.

More, Ax, and Ray Kurzweil. "Max More and Ray Kurzweil on the Singu- larity." February 26, 2002. Accessed March 28, 2015. www.kurzweilai. net/max-more-and-ray-kurzweil-on-the-singularity-2

Musil, Steven. "What Is Geo-Tracking Revealing About You?" CNET. June 17, 2011. Accessed March 29, 2015. www.cnet.com/news /what-is-geo-tracking-revealing-about-you-week-in-review/

Myslewski, Rik. "'Hashtag' Added to the OED – But # Isn't a Hash, Pound, Nor Number Sign." The Register. June 13, 2014. Accessed April 3, 2015. www.theregister.co.uk/2014/06/13/hashtag_added_to_the_oed/.

Nielsen. "Global Advertising Consumers Trust Real Friends and Virtual Strangers the Most." July 7, 2009. Accessed March 28, 2015. www. nielsen.com/us/en/insights/news/2009/global-advertising-consumers -trust-real-friends-and-virtual-strangers-the-most.html.

———. "Nielsen: Global Consumers' Trust in 'Earned' Advertising Grows in Importance." April 10, 2012. Accessed March 28, 2015.

www.nielsen.com/us/en/press-room/2012/neilsen-global-consumers
-trust-in-earned-advertising-grows.html.

Norton, Quinn. "How Anonymous Picks Targets, Launches Attacks, and
Takes Powerful Organizations Down." Wired. August 3, 2012. Accessed
April 5, 2015. www.wired.com/2012/07/ff_anonymous/all/.

Occupy Wall Street NYC General Assembly. "FAQ." Accessed April 3, 2015.
www.nycga.net/resources/faq/.

Ohannessian, Kevin. "Google Lets the Trolls Back on YouTube." Tech
Times. July 16, 2014. Accessed April 3, 2015. www.techtimes.com
/articles/10591/20140716/google-youtube-comments.htm.

Oliphant, Roland and Colin Freeman. "Ukraine Sees Biggest Anti-Gov-
ern¬ment Protests Since Orange Revolution." The Telegraph. December 1, 2013. Accessed March 31, 2015. www.telegraph.co.uk/news
/worldnews/europe/ukraine/10487001/Ukraine-sees-biggest-anti
-government-protests-since-Orange-Revolution.html.

Orwell, George. Nineteen Eighty-Four. London: Secker and Warburg, 1949.

Pachal, Pete. "How the #YesAllWomen Hashtag Began." Mashable.
May 26, 2014. Accessed April 3, 2015. mashable.com/2014/05/26
/yesallwomen-hashtag/.

Paunescu, Delia. "Bill Cosby's Massive Social Media Fail." New York Post.
November 10, 2014. Accessed April 3, 2014. nypost.com/2014/11/10
/bill-cosby-twitter-hasthag-meme-immediately-backfired/.

PCMag. "Definition of: Mobile Positioning." PC Magazine Encyclopedia.
Accessed March 29, 2015. www.pcmag.com/encyclopedia/term/47145
/mobile-positioning

Phillip, Sarah. "A Brief History of Twitter." The Guardian. July 25, 2007.
Accessed March 28, 2015. www.theguardian.com/technology/2001
/jul/25/media.newmedia

Pigareva, Olga. "Prominent Russians: Pavel Durov." Russiapedia. Accessed
March 28, 2015. russiapedia.rt.com/prominent-russians/science
-and-technology/pavel-durov/

Plumridge, Nicole. "Is the Internet Destroying Our Attention Span?"
Psych.com. August 1, 2013. Accessed April 1, 2015. psychminds.com
/is-the-internet-destroying-our-attentions-span/.

Pocket. "Pocket." Accessed April 1, 2015. getpocket.com.

Pogue, David. "Don't Worry About Who's Watching." Scientific American. December 22, 2010. Accessed April 5, 2015. www.scientificamerican. com/article/dont-worry-about-whos-watching/.

Popescu, Adam. "3 Must-Have Geolocation Apps." Mashable. May 9, 2013. Accessed March 29, 2015. mashable.com/2013/05/08/top-geolocation -apps-you-need/

Potter, Ned. "How Chris Hadfield Conquered Social Media from Outer Space." Forbes. June 28, 2013. Accessed March 24, 2015. www.forbes. com/sites/forbesleadershipforum/2013/06/28/how-chris-hadfield -conquered-social-media-from-outer-space/

Potter, Janet. "How Emily Graslie Went from YouTube Science Star to Full-Time at the Field Museum." Chicago Reader. January 27, 2014. Accessed April 6, 2015. www.chicagoreader.com/chicago/field- museum-emily-graslie-brain-scoop-youtube/Content?oid=12236428.

Potter, Will. "Meet the Punk Rocker Who Can Liberate Your FBI File." Mother Jones. November 13, 2013. Accessed April 3, 2015. www. motherjones.com/politics/2013/11/foia-ryan-shapiro-fbi-files-lawsuit.

Poulsen, Kevin. "FBI's Secret Spyware Tracks Down Teen Who Made Bomb Threats." Wired. July 18, 2007. Accessed April 5, 2015. archive.wired. com/politics/law/news/2007/07/fbi_spyware.

Pozin, Ilya. "15 Social Media Companies to Watch in 2015." Forbes. December 17, 2014. Accessed March 28, 2015. www.forbes.com/sites /ilyapozin/2014/12/17/15-social-media-companies-to-watch-in-2015/

PrivCo. "Facebook, Inc." Private Company Financial Intelligence. Accessed April 6, 2015. www.privco.com/private-company/facebook-inc.

PrivCo. "Twitter Inc." Private Company Financial Intelligence. Accessed April 6, 2015. www.privco.com/private-company/twitter-inc.

Radcliffe, Damian. "How People in the Middle East Use Social Media." LinkedIn. May 24, 2014. Accessed April 6, 2015. www.linkedin.com /pulse/20140524190814-11449736-how-people-in-the-middle-east -use-social-media

RallyEngine. "10 Clever Apps that Use Geo-Location." The RallyEngine Blog. May 28, 2013. Accessed March 29, 2015. www.rallyengine.com /blog/bid/273557/10-clever-apps-that-use-geo-location

Rash, Wayne. "Mobile Phone Geo-Tracking Means You Can Run, but You Can't Hide." eWeek. April 25, 2011. Accessed March 29, 2015.

www.eweek.com/c/a/Security/Mobile-Phone-GeoTracking-Means
-You-Can-Run-but-You-Cant-Hide-413631

Richards, Luke. "Stats: Social Media Growth and Impact Across the
Middle East." E-Consultancy. August 8, 2012. Accessed April 6, 2015.
econsultancy.com/blog/10491-stats-social-media-growth-and
-impact-across-the-middle-east/

Rosen, David. "6 Government Surveillance Programs Designed to Watch
What You Do Online." Alternet. June 6, 2012. Accessed March 29,
2015. www.alternet.org/story/155764/6_government_surveillance_
programs_designed_to_watch_what_you_do_online

Rotten Tomatoes. "Rosewater (2014)." Rotten Tomatoes. Accessed April 6,
2015. www.rottentomatoes.com/m/rosewater.

Rouse, Margaret. "White Hat." Tech Target. Accessed April 5, 2015.
searchsecurity.techtarget.com/definition/white-hat.

Ryan, Maureen. "The Threats Against Anita Sarkeesian Expose the Dark-
est Aspects of Online Misogyny." Huffington Post. October 14, 2014.
Accessed April 3, 2015. www.huffingtonpost.com/maureen-ryan
/anita-sarkeesian_b_5993082.html

Sagolla, Dom. "How Twitter Was Born." 140 Characters. January 30, 2009.
Accessed March 28, 2015. www.140characters.com/2009/01/30/how
-twitter-was-born

Sasaki, Darla. "IRC 101: What Is It & How Do I Use It?" The Mac Observer.
April 4, 2002. Accessed April 5, 2015. www.macobserver.com/tip
/2002/04/04.1.shtml

Sauter, Molly. "Guy Fawkes Mask-ology." HiLobrow. April 3, 2012. Accessed
April 5, 2015. hilobrow.com/2012/04/30/mask/.

Schneider, Michael. "New to Your TV Screen: Twitter Hashtags." TV Guide.
April 21, 2011. Accessed April 3, 2015. www.tvguide.com/news/new
-tv-screen-1032111/.

Schwartz, Mattathias. Map: How Occupy Wall Street Chose Zuccotti Park.
The New Yorker. November 18, 2011. Accessed April 3, 2015. www.
newyorker.com/news/news-desk/map-how-occupy-wall-street-chose
-zuccotti-park.

Senior, Jennifer. "Anthony Weiner's Big Ego." New York. June 2, 2011.
Accessed April 5, 2015. nymag.com/daily/intelligencer/2011/06
/anthony_weiners_big_ego.html.

Shane, Scott and Ben Hubbard. "ISIS Displaying a Deft Command of Varied Media." The New York Times. August 30, 2014. Accessed April 1, 2015. www.nytimes.com/2014/08/31/world/middleeast/isis-displaying -a-deft-command-of-varied-media.html.

Shoard, Catherine. "Sony Hack: The Plot to Kill The Interview—A Timeline So Far." The Guardian. December 18, 2014. Accessed April 3, 2015. www. theguardian.com/film/2014/dec/18/sony-hack-the-interview-timeline.

Simpson, John. "Who Are the Winners and Losers from the Arab Spring?" BBC News. November 12, 2014. Accessed March 31, 2015. www.bbc. com/news/world-middle-east-30003865.

Simons, Lewis M. "Can Thailand Avoid Another Coup?" National Geographic. January 2014. Accessed March 31, 2015. news.nationalgeographic.com /news/features/2014/01/140113-thailand-red-yellow-shirts-thaksin -bhumibol-insurgency-bangkok-world/.

SiteGround. "Google Sponsored Search Programs." Accessed March 28, 2015. www.siteground.com/tutorials/sem/google_sponsored_search.htm.

Shu, Catherine. "Meet Telegram, a Secure Messaging App from the Found-ers of VK, Russia's Largest Social Network." TechCrunch. October 27, 2013. Accessed March 28, 2015. techcrunch.com/2013/10/27/meet -telegram-a-secure-messaging-app-from-the-founders-of-vk-russias -largest-social-network/

Statista. "Leading Social Networks Worldwide as of March 2015, Ranked by Number of Active Users (in Millions)." Accessed March 30, 2015. www.statista.com/statistics/272014/global-social-networks-ranked -by-number-of-users/.

TBI Reporter. "Comment: How Social Media Is Influencing Reality Development." Television Business International. October 24, 2013. Accessed April 6, 2015. tbivision.com/features/2013/10/comment -how-social-media-is-influencing-reality-development/170252/.

TechTerms.com. "Trojan Horse." Accessed April 5, 2015. techterms.com /definition/trojanhorse.

The Telegraph Foreign Staff. "Ukraine Crisis Timeline of Major Events." The Telegraph. March 5, 2015. Accessed March 31, 2015. www.telegraph. co.uk/news/worldnews/europe/ukraine/11449122/Ukraine-crisis -timeline-of-major-events.html.

The Weather Channel. "Photos and Video." Accessed April 1, 2015.
www.weather.com/photos.

The Weather Network. "Community." Accessed April 1, 2015. www.
theweathernetwork.com/community.

Ungerleider, Neal. "Afghanistan's Amazing DIY Internet." Fast Company.
June 11, 2011. Accessed April 1, 2015. www.fastcompany.com/1761891
/afghanistans-amazing-diy-internet.

Torr, Donné. "Here Are 7 Movies and 1 TV Series Every Social Media Man-
ager Should Watch." Hootsuite. January 2015. Accessed April 6, 2015.
blog.hootsuite.com/movies-for-social-media-managers/.

Tracy, Abigail. "Beyoncé Shows How Social Media Is Changing Marketing."
Inc. December 16, 2013. Accessed April 6, 2015. www.inc.com/abigail
-tracy/beyonce-shows-the-true-power-of-social-media.html.

Twitter. "Twitter Privacy Policy." Last updated September 8, 2014. Accessed
April 5, 2015. twitter.com/privacy?lang=en.

———. "Using Hashtags on Twitter." Twitter Help Center. Accessed April 3,
2015. support.twitter.com/articles/49309-using-hashtags-on-twitter.

Tweney, Dylan. "Facebook Is Blowing It with Its 'Real Name' Policy."
Venture Beat. February 12, 2015. Accessed April 5, 2015.

US Department of Justice. "Eleven Defendants Indicted on Domestic
Terrorism Charges." January 20, 2006. Accessed March 30, 2015.
www.justice.gov/archive/opa/pr/2006/January/06_crm_030.html.

———. "The USA PATRIOT Act: Preserving Life and Liberty." Accessed
March 29, 2015. www.justice.gov/archive/ll/highlights.htm

Vamosi, Robert. "Pirated Movies: Now Playing on a Server Near You."
ZD Net. May 8, 2002. Accessed April 5, 2015. www.zdnet.com/article
/pirated-movies-now-playing-on-a-server-near-you/.

Vinge, Vernor. "The Coming Technological Singularity: How to Survive in
the Post-Human Era." VISION-2 Symposium. March 30-31, 1993. NASA
Lewis Research Center and Ohio Aerospace Institute. Accessed March
28, 2015.www-rohan.sdsu.edu/faculty/vinge/misc/singularity.html.

Weatherhead, Rob. "Say It Quick, Say It Well: The Attention Span of
a Modern Internet Consumer." The Guardian. February 28, 2014.
Accessed April 1, 2015. www.theguardian.com/media-network/media
-network-blog/2012/mar/19/attention-span-internet-consumer.

"What Are Hashflags?" Accessed April 3, 2015. howto.digidefen.se/twitter
/What-are-hashflags.php.

Daily Planet Official Website. Accessed April 1, 2015. www.discovery.ca
/Shows/Daily-Planet.

WikiLeaks. "About: What Is WikiLeaks?" Accessed April 5, 2015. wikileaks.
org/About.html.

Williams, Ev. "How @replies Work on Twitter (and How They Might)."
Twitter Blog. May 12, 2008. Accessed April 3, 2015. blog.twitter.
com/2008/how-replies-work-twitter-and-how-they-might.

Wolf, Paul, et al. COINTELPRO: The Untold American Story. 2001. Accessed
March 30, 2015. archive.org/details/CointelproTheUntoldAmericanStory.

Woolf, Nicky. "Best Buy Forced to Apologise for 'Insensitive' Serial Tweet."
The Guardian. December 12, 2014. Accessed April 3, 2015. www.
theguardian.com/tv-and-radio/2014/dec/11/best-buy-apology
-serial-tweet.

WYSK. "#InMyShoes: Scientists Show Off Their Footwear on Twitter
in Support of 8-Year-Old Girl Denied Dinosaur Shoes." Women
You Should Know. March 19, 2015. Accessed April 3, 2015.
www.womenyoushouldknow.net/inmyshoes-scientists-show-off
-their-footwear-on-twitter-in-support-of-8-year-old-girl-denied
-dinosaur-shoes/.

George Takei on Facebook. www.facebook.com/georgehtakei.

Neil deGrasse Tyson on Twitter. twitter.com/neiltyson.

The Brain Scoop on YouTube. www.youtube.com/user/thebrainscoop.

INDEX

CONTINUE THE
CONVERSATION

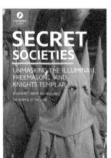

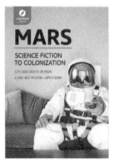

DISCOVER MORE AT

www.lightningguides.com/books

CPSIA information can be obtained at www.ICGtesting.com
Printed in the USA
BVOW11s2217280515

402313BV00001B/1/P

9 781942 411444